Celebrating Sunday
for Catholic
Families
2018–2019

Kerstin Keber Smith

LITURGY
TRAINING
PUBLICATIONS

Nihil Obstat
Reverend Mr. Brian G. Welter, JD
Chancellor
Archdiocese of Chicago
September 26, 2017

Imprimatur
Very Reverend Ronald A. Hicks
Vicar General
Archdiocese of Chicago
September 26, 2017

The *Nihil Obstat* and *Imprimatur* are declarations that the material is free from doctrinal or moral error, and thus is granted permission to publish in accordance with c. 827. No legal responsibility is assumed by the grant of this permission. No implication is contained herein that those who have granted the *Nihil Obstat* and *Imprimatur* agree with the content, opinions, or statements expressed.

CELEBRATING SUNDAY FOR CATHOLIC FAMILIES 2018–2019 © 2018 Archdiocese of Chicago: Liturgy Training Publications, 3949 South Racine Avenue, Chicago, IL 60609; 800-933-1800; fax 800-933-7094; e-mail: orders@ltp.org; website: www.LTP.org. All rights reserved.

This book was edited by Mary Fox. Christian Rocha was the production editor, Anna Manhart was the designer, and Kari Nicholls was the production artist.

Cover illustration by Eleanor Davis © LTP.

Printed in the United States of America.

ISBN 978-1-61671-384-3

CSCF19

"You shall love the LORD your God with all your heart, and with all your soul, and with all your might. Keep these words that I am commanding to you today in your heart. Recite them to your children and talk about them when you are at home and when you are away, when you lie down and when you rise."

(Deuteronomy 6:5–7)

Contents

How to Use

Celebrating Sunday for Catholic Families

This small weekly guide draws on the Gospel for each Sunday and Holyday for the coming year. It is intended to help parents engage their children with the Mass and deepen their appreciation of the richness of their faith life. So often, going to Mass becomes a weekly event that begins and ends at the church door. The brief reflection for the parent on an excerpt from the Gospel is intended to spark his or her thinking about the Scripture that will lead to conversation with the family on the way to and from Mass. Suggestions for questions and conversation starters are provided, as well as some practice or practical way to carry this reflection into the life of the family.

We hope that many of the reflections and suggestions will enrich your family's life of faith. Some weeks, you may have other needs, concerns, or ideas that fit your life. If so, engage your children with those. A note about very young children: they are very able to enter into the liturgy through their senses. Singing the hymns, calling their attention to the changing colors of the liturgical seasons, and sitting where they can observe the gestures of the Mass are all ways to form them in the faith. Always remember, as the Rite of Baptism proclaims, you, as parents, are your children's first and most important teachers.

September 9, 2018

Twenty-Third Sunday in Ordinary Time

Hearing the Word

Mark 7:31–37

In the name of the Father, and of the Son, and of the Holy Spirit.

Again Jesus left the district of Tyre, and went by way of Sidon to the Sea of Galilee, into the district of Decapolis. And people brought to him a deaf man who had a speech impediment and begged him to lay his hand on him. He took him off by himself away from the crowd. He put his finger into the man's ears and, spitting, touched his tongue; then he looked up to heaven and groaned, and said to him, "*Ephphatha!*"—that is, "Be opened!"—And immediately the man's ears were opened, his speech impediment was removed, and he spoke plainly. He ordered them not to tell anyone. But the more he ordered them not to, the more they proclaimed it. They were exceedingly astonished and they said, "He has done all things well. He makes the deaf hear and the mute speak."

Reflecting on the Word

"Be opened!" When we are open, we enter a relationship, a text, or a situation without preconceived ideas or attitudes. At these times, we allow a person, language, or an event in without judgment. When we are open, we make room for others and new thoughts and experiences. At these times, we also allow God to work in us and through us. As children begin a new school year, parents can help them to be open to what awaits them. Only through their being open will they allow new people, perspectives, and ideas to enrich them. Though adults may feel that they have traveled a path before, they need to be open to the new ways God can work within them. What was once thought to be permanent (like deafness in the man) may change.

•••••• ON THE WAY TO MASS

Where in your life have you been closed off and needed to be more open?

ON THE WAY HOME FROM MASS ••••••

How does it feel when you think about being more open? What kinds of emotions come up?

Living the Word

As a family, take a walk down your street. Invite each family member to look at the neighborhood with new eyes, as though they had never been on the street before. Do they see anything that they has gone unnoticed? When the family gets home, encourage each person to count the number of things that were seen with new eyes. How did it feel to be open to seeing new things in their neighborhood? What difference would it make to always be open to God?

September 16, 2018

Twenty-Fourth Sunday in Ordinary Time

Hearing the Word

Mark 8:27–35

In the name of the Father, and of the Son, and of the Holy Spirit.

Jesus and his disciples set out for the villages of Caesarea Philippi. Along the way he asked his disciples, "Who do people say that I am?" They said in reply, "John the Baptist, others Elijah, still others one of the prophets." And he asked them, "But who do you say that I am?" Peter said to him in reply, "You are the Christ." Then he warned them not to tell anyone about him.

He began to teach them that the Son of Man must suffer greatly and be rejected by the elders, the chief priests, and the scribes, and be killed, and rise after three days. He spoke this openly. Then Peter took him aside and began to rebuke him. At this he turned around and, looking at his disciples, rebuked Peter and said, "Get behind me, Satan. You are thinking not as God does, but as human beings do."

He summoned the crowd with his disciples and said to them, "Whoever wishes to come after me must deny himself, take up his cross, and follow me. For whoever wishes to save his life will lose it, but whoever loses his life for my sake and that of the gospel will save it."

Reflecting on the Word

When we lose ourselves to the deep transformative love of God, we gain an entire world of understanding, compassion, and wisdom. Only by letting go of our attachments can we relinquish ourselves to God. During the times that we cling to the past, there is no space for God to come into our lives, and our humanity limits us. Losing our life for the sake of Jesus and the Gospel is the only way we can truly save it for all eternity with God.

•••••• ON THE WAY TO MASS

Where can you let God into your life more?

ON THE WAY HOME FROM MASS ••••••

What is your favorite name that people call you? What would you like to be called?

Living the Word

Ask your family to list some of the names Jesus is called in this Scripture passage as well as names Jesus is called in other places in the Bible. Next, request that the family make up a few names for Jesus that have meaning for them. Invite each person to pick a favorite name from the list, and share why they are attracted to it. Try incorporating some of these names into your daily prayer (for example, Jesus, loving teacher, be with us as we start our school day).

September 23, 2018

Twenty-Fifth Sunday in Ordinary Time

Hearing the Word

Mark 9:30–37

In the name of the Father, and of the Son, and of the Holy Spirit.

Jesus and his disciples left from there and began a journey through Galilee, but he did not wish anyone to know about it. He was teaching his disciples and telling them, "The Son of Man is to be handed over to men and they will kill him, and three days after his death the Son of Man will rise." But they did not understand the saying and they were afraid to question him.

They came to Capernaum and, once inside the house, he began to ask them, "What were you arguing about on the way?" But they remained silent. They had been discussing among themselves on the way who was the greatest. Then he sat down, called the Twelve, and said to them, "If anyone wishes to be first, he shall be the last of all and the servant of all." Taking a child, he placed it in their midst, and putting his arms around it, he said to them, "Whoever receives one child such as this in my name, receives me; and whoever receives me, receives not me but the One who sent me."

Reflecting on the Word

We come from God and so shall we return. Our lives are an expression of God's love. Within that love, there is no greatest or least nor first or last; all is simply love. A way to express our love for God is by loving the person next to us. We are called to love all the many and varied expressions of God's love in the world, even the ones we find hardest to love.

•••••• ON THE WAY TO MASS

How can you show kindness to other children?

ON THE WAY HOME FROM MASS ••••••

Why would the person who wishes to be first be last? Why would that person serve others?

Living the Word

Invite your children to spend some time playing with a balloon, expanding and contracting it and letting each family member experiment with it. Then, on a deflated balloon, draw a small heart in permanent marker and color it in. Explain that we are like the balloon with the small heart, and at times we may not seem to be much, but when we allow in God or *ruah*—breath, wind, and spirit as God is called in the Old Testament (blow into the balloon)—we are so much bigger.

September 30, 2018

Twenty-Sixth Sunday in Ordinary Time

Hearing the Word

Mark 9:38–43, 45, 47–48

In the name of the Father, and of the Son, and of the Holy Spirit.

At that time, John said to Jesus, "Teacher, we saw someone driving out demons in your name, and we tried to prevent him because he does not follow us." Jesus replied, "Do not prevent him. There is no one who performs a mighty deed in my name who can at the same time speak ill of me. For whoever is not against us is for us. Anyone who gives you a cup of water to drink because you belong to Christ, amen, I say to you, will surely not lose his reward.

"Whoever causes one of these little ones who believe in me to sin, it would be better for him if a great millstone were put around his neck and he were thrown into the sea. If your hand causes you to sin, cut it off. It is better for you to enter into life maimed than with two hands to go into Gehenna, into the unquenchable fire. And if your foot causes you to sin, cut it off. It is better for you to enter into life crippled than with two feet to be thrown into Gehenna. And if your eye causes you to sin, pluck it out. Better for you to enter into the kingdom of God with one eye than with two eyes to be thrown into Gehenna, where 'their worm does not die, and the fire is not quenched.'"

Reflecting on the Word

What is valuable in the eyes of the Lord? What we often think is important is not as valuable as our relationship with God. Spending energy maintaining an appearance of a full and happy life but not living one is useless. Doing so is like having two hands that harm versus one doing good. Consider where your family places energy and focus. It matters not that perfection was attained. God's love is what matters. Our focus should be on how we spread that love by extending mercy and forgiveness.

••••••ON THE WAY TO MASS

Can you imagine being without an eye, hand, or foot? What importance do those hold for you?

ON THE WAY HOME FROM MASS ••••••

Have you ever been surprised by someone's kindness? Why did it surprise you?

Living the Word

Ask family members to reflect on their strengths and weaknesses. When are they tempted to do wrong? In what situations are they good at doing the right thing? For instance, are they kind to someone others exclude? How can they strengthen the parts in their lives that are weak?

October 7, 2018

Twenty-Seventh Sunday in Ordinary Time

Hearing the Word

Mark 10:2–9, 13–16

In the name of the Father, and of the Son, and of the Holy Spirit.

The Pharisees approached Jesus and asked, "Is it lawful for a husband to divorce his wife?" . . . He said to them in reply, "What did Moses command you?" They replied, "Moses permitted a husband to write a bill of divorce and dismiss her." But Jesus told them, "Because of the hardness of your hearts he wrote you this commandment. But from the beginning of creation, *God made them male and female. For this reason a man shall leave his father and mother and be joined to his wife, and the two shall become one flesh.* So they are no longer two but one flesh. Therefore what God has joined together, no human being must separate."

And people were bringing children to [Jesus] that he might touch them, but the disciples rebuked them. When Jesus saw this he became indignant and said to them, "Let the children come to me; do not prevent them, for the kingdom of God belongs to such as these. Amen, I say to you, whoever does not accept the kingdom of God like a child will not enter it." Then he embraced them and blessed them, placing his hands on them.

Reflecting on the Word

The beginning of a family is a holy time. Surrounded by a community of support, two people come together and join their lives. The holiness and grace within that act of commitment can never be undone. Jesus, however, cautions that family members should be careful not to harden their hearts to one another. Every day this commitment is a choice a family makes over and over again.

•••••• ON THE WAY TO MASS

What do you know about the day your parents married? What else would you like to know about that day?

ON THE WAY HOME FROM MASS ••••••

Pick something to look at with the eyes of a child younger than you, what does it look like?

Living the Word

Tell the children about St. Francis of Assisi, whose memorial was celebrated on October 4. Explain to them that St. Francis was known for preaching with his life. He even preached to the birds and all of creation through his gentle deeds and actions. With your children, take time today to preach with your life to the small or forgotten. Perhaps the children will want to hang a bird feeder, help a younger child, or send a note or drawing to a grandparent. Let the children know that these actions make the Gospel alive.

October 14, 2018

Twenty-Eighth Sunday in Ordinary Time

Hearing the Word

Mark 10:17–22

In the name of the Father, and of the Son, and of the Holy Spirit.

As Jesus was setting out on a journey, a man ran up, knelt down before him, and asked him, "Good teacher, what must I do to inherit eternal life?" Jesus answered him, "Why do you call me good? No one is good but God alone. You know the commandments: *You shall not kill; you shall not commit adultery; you shall not steal; you shall not bear false witness; you shall not defraud; honor your father and your mother.*" He replied and said to him, "Teacher, all of these I have observed from my youth." Jesus, looking at him, loved him and said to him, "You are lacking in one thing. Go, sell what you have, and give to the poor and you will have treasure in heaven; then come, follow me." At that statement his face fell and he went away sad, for he had many possessions.

Reflecting on the Word

This can be a hard Gospel to apply to our lives. Most of us have many possessions; some of these are necessary. How could God call us to give up everything? Perhaps you might want to consider if there is anything that keeps you from your relationship with God. Is there anything that you depend on more than you depend on God? That is what you would need to give up.

•••••• ON THE WAY TO MASS

What have you put before your love for Jesus? What is holding you back from following him fully?

ON THE WAY HOME FROM MASS ••••••

Where could you make more room for God in your life? How would that feel?

Living the Word

Encourage your family to consider what they could give up for a week to make space for God as a family together. Perhaps instead of watching TV in the evening, cards could be written to parishioners who are sick. Or the family might want to pray the Rosary in the car instead of listening to the radio or make a dessert for the homeless shelter. The time also might be spent going through the house and reducing possessions. Notice how this exercise shifts the attention of the family.

October 21, 2018

Twenty-Ninth Sunday in Ordinary Time

Hearing the Word

Mark 10:35–45

In the name of the Father, and of the Son, and of the Holy Spirit.

James and John, the sons of Zebedee, came to Jesus and said to him, "Teacher, we want you to do for us whatever we ask of you." He replied, "What do you wish me to do for you?" They answered him, "Grant that in your glory we may sit one at your right and the other at your left." Jesus said to them, "You do not know what you are asking. Can you drink the cup that I drink or be baptized with the baptism with which I am baptized?" They said to him, "We can." Jesus said to them, "The cup that I drink, you will drink and with the baptism with which I am baptized, you will be baptized; but to sit at my right or at my left is not mine to give but is for those for whom it has been prepared." When the ten heard this, they became indignant at James and John. Jesus summoned them and said to them, "You know that those who are recognized as rulers over the Gentiles lord it over them, and their great ones make their authority over them felt. But it shall not be so among you. Rather, whoever wishes to be great among you will be your servant; whoever wishes to be first among you will be the slave of all. For the Son of Man did not come to be served but to serve and to give his life as a ransom for many."

Reflecting on the Word

In today's Gospel, Jesus introduces his followers to what we think of today as servant leadership. The leadership that the disciples are to embrace calls them to serve others. Those who follow the way of the Lord will not be lauded for their greatness. Instead, they will humble themselves to serve others. By doing so, they will drink the cup that Jesus drinks.

······ ON THE WAY TO MASS

Whom do you see as a leader? What have they done to show you this?

ON THE WAY HOME FROM MASS ······

What are some things James and John did not know when they said they would gladly be just like Jesus?

Living the Word

Gather the family and ask them to consider serving each other this week. Each family member could pick a day to be the leader in service. This leader would spend the day performing simple tasks for the rest of the family. These tasks could be holding the door, doing the dishes, or tidying up. At the end of the week, gather to reflect on the services each person performed and how it felt to serve and be served. Did family members find it felt good to serve others?

October 28, 2018

Thirtieth Sunday in Ordinary Time

Hearing the Word

Mark 10:46–52

In the name of the Father, and of the Son, and of the Holy Spirit.

As Jesus was leaving Jericho with his disciples and a sizable crowd, Bartimaeus, a blind man, the son of Timaeus, sat by the roadside begging. On hearing that it was Jesus of Nazareth, he began to cry out and say, "Jesus, son of David, have pity on me." And many rebuked him, telling him to be silent. But he kept calling out all the more, "Son of David, have pity on me." Jesus stopped and said, "Call him." So they called the blind man, saying to him, "Take courage; get up, Jesus is calling you." He threw aside his cloak, sprang up, and came to Jesus. Jesus said to him in reply, "What do you want me to do for you?" The blind man replied to him, "Master, I want to see." Jesus told him, "Go your way; your faith has saved you." Immediately he received his sight and followed him on the way.

Reflecting on the Word

Jesus does not claim glory for his miracles but repeatedly points out the role of faith in healing. We will never be whole, healed, or anything but broken if we don't believe we can be. Our divine origins are often beyond our imagination, but if we dare to see with the eyes of faith, we discover the limitlessness of our lives. Healing is simply returning home to the person God made us to be from the very beginning.

••••••ON THE WAY TO MASS

What would you like God to heal in your life? Why do you think it would be possible?

ON THE WAY HOME FROM MASS ••••••

Which of your five senses are you most thankful for? Why?

Living the Word

Play a family board game together, preferably one that uses many of your senses. Invite family members to take turns playing the game without the use of sight, touch, voice, or whatever may be appropriate for the game. Each person only forgoes the sense on his or her turn, and other family members can provide needed help. Discuss what it would be like to live without one of your senses and what it would feel like to have it suddenly restored, as happened in the Gospel.

November 1, 2018

Solemnity of All Saints

Hearing the Word
Matthew 5:1–12a

In the name of the Father, and of the Son, and of the Holy Spirit.

When Jesus saw the crowds, he went up the mountain, and after he had sat down, his disciples came to him. He began to teach them, saying: / "Blessed are the poor in spirit, / for theirs is the Kingdom of heaven. / Blessed are they who mourn, / for they will be comforted. / Blessed are the meek, / for they will inherit the land. / Blessed are they who hunger and thirst for righteousness, / for they will be satisfied. / Blessed are the merciful, / for they will be shown mercy. / Blessed are the clean of heart, / for they will see God. / Blessed are the peacemakers, / for they will be called children of God. / Blessed are they who are persecuted for the sake of righteousness, / for theirs is the Kingdom of heaven. / Blessed are you when they insult you and persecute you / and utter every kind of evil against you falsely because of me. / Rejoice and be glad, / for your reward will be great in heaven."

Reflecting on the Word

It can seem that the Beatitudes contradict our experience of the world. After all, when do we see the meek inheriting anything? Often, too, peacemakers are not regarded well. But the Beatitudes look to God's Kingdom and show what God holds as important. The poor in spirit rely on God, so the Kingdom of Heaven will be theirs. It can be hard to model our lives after the poor, the meek, and the persecuted, for we long for an earthly reward. In the Beatitudes, Jesus puts the way of God and the way of heaven before us.

•••••• ON THE WAY TO MASS

What is a reward that may seem good at first but not helpful in the long run?

ON THE WAY HOME FROM MASS ••••••

What are some of the blessings in your life?

Living the Word

Invite each person in the family to state their favorite Beatitude, an attitude that goes with it, and three examples of how to live it. For instance, the attitude of the meek is one of service. That attitude can be taken on through acts of kindness and compassion. Family members, then, choose one of the acts to be their respective Beatitude mission this week and make the accompanying attitude theirs for a day. When complete, all share how they felt "blessed" with their new Beatitude attitude.

November 4, 2018

Thirty-First Sunday in Ordinary Time

Hearing the Word

Mark 12:38b–34

In the name of the Father, and of the Son, and of the Holy Spirit.

One of the scribes came to Jesus and asked him, "Which is the first of all the commandments?" Jesus replied, "The first is this: *Hear, O Israel! The Lord our God is Lord alone! You shall love the Lord your God with all your heart, with all your soul, with all your mind, and with all your strength.* The second is this: *You shall love your neighbor as yourself.* There is no other commandment greater than these." The scribe said to him, "Well said, teacher. You are right in saying, 'He is One and there is no other than he.' And 'to love him with all your heart, with all your understanding, with all your strength, and to love your neighbor as yourself' is worth more than all burnt offerings and sacrifices." And when Jesus saw that he answered with understanding, he said to him, "You are not far from the kingdom of God." And no one dared to ask him any more questions.

Reflecting on the Word

When the scribe asked which Commandment was first, Jesus' answer showed that God demands nothing less than our whole selves. Jesus said that we are to love with our whole heart, mind, soul, and strength. In other words, we can leave no part of our being out of loving God. If we allow distractions to our faith, our heart will be filled with other loves rather than God. The masters of time, wealth, power, and prestige are fickle and always want more. When we love God with our whole heart, and through that, ourselves and our neighbors, we will find that God will fill us with love.

......ON THE WAY TO MASS

What false master have you allowed to rule your heart?
What happened?

ON THE WAY HOME FROM MASS ......

What would it feel like to love God with your whole heart?
What is stopping you?

Living the Word

A heart divided is never full. Invite each family member to cut out a large heart and write all the things they love on it. Name people, activities, things, and whatever else takes up their time. Cut the heart into pieces, with one item per piece. After mixing up the pieces, put the heart back together. Notice the cracks and how the heart doesn't hold its shape as well. Now make one big heart for the whole family and write *God* on it. Paste everyone's pieces in it. When God holds everything, we can find wholeness again through that love.

November 11, 2018

Thirty-Second Sunday in Ordinary Time

Hearing the Word

Mark 12:38–44

In the name of the Father, and of the Son, and of the Holy Spirit.

In the course of his teaching Jesus said to the crowds, "Beware of the scribes, who like to go around in long robes and accept greetings in the marketplaces, seats of honor in synagogues, and places of honor at banquets. They devour the houses of widows and, as a pretext recite lengthy prayers. They will receive a very severe condemnation."

He sat down opposite the treasury and observed how the crowd put money into the treasury. Many rich people put in large sums. A poor widow also came and put in two small coins worth a few cents. Calling his disciples to himself, he said to them, "Amen, I say to you, this poor widow put in more than all the other contributors to the treasury. For they have all contributed from their surplus wealth, but she, from her poverty, has contributed all she had, her whole livelihood."

Reflecting on the Word

How do you envision holiness? Today's Gospel portrays a holy woman as someone who contributed all she had. That leaves us with the question of what we return to God. Is your life focused on what God wants, or do you reserve a certain amount of time and space for God? God has given us our lives. Our only return is a life centered on God.

. . . . . . ON THE WAY TO MASS

How would you describe holiness?

ON THE WAY HOME FROM MASS . . . . . .

How do you support your church? What kinds of time, talent, and treasure do you share?

Living the Word

As a family, pick one activity from your church bulletin to participate in this week or to donate to. This may require skipping a routine or giving up something. Just like the widow that gave out of her need, help your family determine how to be more intentional about giving back to your church community. If possible, the family might purposely choose a time or way that is inconvenient. This can show a commitment to the parish community.

Thirty-Third Sunday in Ordinary Time

Hearing the Word

Mark 13:24–32

In the name of the Father, and of the Son, and of the Holy Spirit.

Jesus said to his disciples: "In those days after that tribulation the sun will be darkened, and the moon will not give its light, and the stars will be falling from the sky, and the powers in the heavens will be shaken.

"And then they will see 'the Son of Man coming in the clouds' with great power and glory, and then he will send out the angels and gather his elect from the four winds, from the end of the earth to the end of the sky.

"Learn a lesson from the fig tree. When its branch becomes tender and sprouts leaves, you know that summer is near. In the same way, when you see these things happening, know that he is near, at the gates. Amen, I say to you, this generation will not pass away until all these things have taken place. Heaven and earth will pass away, but my words will not pass away.

"But of that day or hour, no one knows, neither the angels in heaven, nor the Son, but only the Father."

Reflecting on the Word

The images in today's reading are quite dramatic. Daily life is dramatic, too, if we try to see occurrences with the eyes of God. In many ways, Jesus' return will not be so different from any other day. When we choose to see the miracles all around us—from the tiny sprouts of the fig tree to the rising of the sun to the very breath being taken in during this moment—we see signs and wonders all around us. It is possible to live as if Jesus is among us now.

......ON THE WAY TO MASS

What do you think Jesus' return will be like? How will you know he is coming?

ON THE WAY HOME FROM MASS ......

What do you consider a miracle? Why?

Living the Word

Invite your family to go on a miracle scavenger hunt. Make a list of the little signs and wonders that surround you every day, and then go out in teams to witness them. Leave several blank spots on the hunt for the little things that may surprise you along the way when you are looking for wonder. Gather back together to share your lists and discuss what it was like to look at the world with eyes of wonder and awe. Did things look differently? Was there anything that was noticed that normally might have been missed?

Solemnity of Our Lord Jesus Christ, King of the Universe

Hearing the Word

John 18:33b–37

In the name of the Father, and of the Son, and of the Holy Spirit.

Pilate said to Jesus, "Are you the King of the Jews?" Jesus answered, "Do you say this on your own or have others told you about me?" Pilate answered, "I am not a Jew, am I? Your own nation and the chief priests handed you over to me. What have you done?" Jesus answered, "My kingdom does not belong to this world. If my kingdom did belong to this world, my attendants would be fighting to keep me from being handed over to the Jews. But as it is, my kingdom is not here." So Pilate said to him, "Then you are a king?" Jesus answered, "You say I am a king. For this I was born and for this I came into the world, to testify to the truth. Everyone who belongs to the truth listens to my voice."

Reflecting on the Word

The title "King of the Universe" goes so far beyond our small lives that we can barely grasp the immensity of it. Jesus came not just for the sins of humankind but to redeem all of creation and bring the entire cosmos back into God's embrace. Biblical miracles are just the beginning of the awesomeness of a God who wants to be among us. This is a God who reigns over the moon and stars just as tenderly as the bees and flowers. Today's solemnity can help us realize the importance of extending love beyond the immediacy of our short lives and care for creation as God desires.

......ON THE WAY TO MASS

What are some things you know about the universe? How do you care for all of God's creation?

ON THE WAY HOME FROM MASS ......

What does a good king do, say, and look like?

Living the Word

With your family, put on a royal dinner and dress, speak, and eat as if all of you are royalty. During this special occasion, discuss how through Baptism we are at once prophet, priest, and king/queen. As kings/queens we are called to be good stewards of the earth and take care of it. See how little waste you can create with this meal. From using cloth napkins and items that require less packaging or none at all, to conserving water, notice the cosmic impact you can make through simple acts.

December 2, 2018

First Sunday of Advent

Hearing the Word
Luke 21:25–28, 34–36

In the name of the Father, and of the Son, and of the Holy Spirit.

Jesus said to his disciples: "There will be signs in the sun, the moon, and the stars, and on earth nations will be in dismay, perplexed by the roaring of the sea and the waves. People will die of fright in anticipation of what is coming upon the world, for the powers of the heavens will be shaken. And then they will see the Son of Man coming in a cloud with power and great glory. But when these signs begin to happen, stand erect and raise your heads because your redemption is at hand.

"Beware that your hearts do not become drowsy from carousing and drunkenness and the anxieties of daily life, and that day catch you by surprise like a trap. For that day will assault everyone who lives on the face of the earth. Be vigilant at all times and pray that you have the strength to escape the tribulations that are imminent and to stand before the Son of Man."

Reflecting on the Word

In the end, all return to God and are made equal in God's sight. Still, we spend most of our lives building up mountains of work, accomplishments, and awards that will someday be no higher than the valleys we tower over. During Advent, we might consider how we can raise up others in our workplace, community, and home. As we do this, we will be building up the Kingdom of God and straightening paths.

•••••• ON THE WAY TO MASS

What is that unfair thing in the world that you would like to correct?

ON THE WAY HOME FROM MASS ••••••

Is there anything that feels like a mountain weighing you down? Could anyone help you with it?

Living the Word

By the Second Sunday of Advent, family members may feel anxious from the intensity of the preparations for Christmas. After a family member lights the second candle on your Advent wreath, ask each person to sit quietly and focus on his or her breath. Tell them, as they inhale, to slowly breathe in peace and with a sense of resting in God. As they slowly exhale, they can breathe out all the anxiety, worries, and busyness that may surround them. Direct the family to breathe in and out a few times. End the exercise by praying for peace.

December 16, 2018

Third Sunday of Advent

Hearing the Word
Luke 3:10–18

In the name of the Father, and of the Son, and of the Holy Spirit.

The crowds asked John the Baptist, "What should we do?" He said to them in reply, "Whoever has two cloaks should share with the person who has none. And whoever has food should do likewise." Even tax collectors came to be baptized and they said to him, "Teacher, what should we do?" He answered them, "Stop collecting more than what is prescribed." Soldiers also asked him, "And what is it that we should do?" He told them, "Do not practice extortion, do not falsely accuse anyone, and be satisfied with your wages."

Now all the people were filled with expectation, and all were asking in their hearts whether John might be the Christ. John answered them all, saying, "I am baptizing you with water, but one mightier than I is coming. I am not worthy to loosen the thongs of his sandals. He will baptize you with the Holy Spirit and fire. His winnowing fan is in his hand to clear his threshing floor and to gather the wheat into his barn, but the chaff he will burn with unquenchable fire." Exhorting them in many other ways, he preached good news to the people.

Reflecting on the Word

"What should we do?" people ask today when confronted with the concerns of the day. No action can cure all the violence or comfort all mourners. But an individual's concern can warm another's heart and lift burdens. Not only do we give of our cloak for heat but also our smiles and kindness. This warmth keeps us hopeful in times of dark and cold. When all around us grows dim, we look to Christ, whose light we share with others. Once shared, the light continues to grow until, with Christ's coming, we emerge from the shadows.

......ON THE WAY TO MASS

What kind of light brings you the most joy? How do you share that with others?

ON THE WAY HOME FROM MASS ......

Why is the candle this Sunday pink while the others are purple?

Living the Word

As a family member lights the third candle of your Advent wreath, rejoice in the warmth and joy of family. Encourage family members to share something that brought them joy today. Invite them to pause each day this week to think of something for which they are grateful and to thank God for it. Enjoy a family hug.

December 23, 2018

Fourth Sunday of Advent

Hearing the Word
Luke 1:39–45

In the name of the Father, and of the Son, and of the Holy Spirit.

Mary set out and traveled to the hill country in haste to a town of Judah, where she entered the house of Zechariah and greeted Elizabeth. When Elizabeth heard Mary's greeting, the infant leaped in her womb, and Elizabeth, filled with the Holy Spirit, cried out in a loud voice and said, "Blessed are you among women, and blessed is the fruit of your womb. And how does this happen to me, that the mother of my Lord should come to me? For at the moment the sound of your greeting reached my ears, the infant in my womb leaped for joy. Blessed are you who believed that what was spoken to you by the Lord would be fulfilled."

Reflecting on the Word

Theotokos, God bearer, is one of Mary's many names of honor. Mary was so holy that even Elizabeth's baby recognizes from the womb that Jesus was within this young woman. Mary was chosen to carry Jesus because of the holiness that was deep within her. Her life is a testament to the power and beauty of absolute faith and humility. With strength and determination, she cultivated an inner and outer world of blessings.

• • • • • • ON THE WAY TO MASS

What gift do you carry within yourself that others can see lived out in your life?

ON THE WAY HOME FROM MASS • • • • • •

What were the decorations like during Advent? How will they change for Christmas Time?

Living the Word

After the lighting of the fourth candle on the Advent wreath, tell the family that today's Gospel story of the Visitation is the second of the five Joyful Mysteries of the Rosary. Pray one Hail Mary. Tell the children that the other Joyful Mysteries are the Annunciation, the Nativity, the Presentation in the Temple, and the Finding of Jesus in the Temple. Ask the children why they think these are called the Joyful Mysteries. Tell them that the other Mysteries are called the Luminous, Sorrowful, and Glorious. Together, say one Hail Mary for each of the Joyful Mysteries.

December 25, 2018

SOLEMNITY OF THE NATIVITY OF THE LORD

Hearing the Word

Luke 2:15–20

In the name of the Father, and of the Son, and of the Holy Spirit.

When the angels went away from them to heaven,
the shepherds said to one another, "Let us go, then, to
Bethlehem to see this thing that has taken place, which
the Lord has made known to us." So they went in haste and
found Mary and Joseph, and the infant lying in the manger.
When they saw this, they made known the message that
had been told them about this child. All who heard it were
amazed by what had been told them by the shepherds.
And Mary kept all these things, reflecting on them in
her heart. Then the shepherds returned, glorifying and
praising God for all they had heard and seen, just as it
had been told to them.

Reflecting on the Word

On this joyful day, we celebrate that God cared for us enough to send his Son. Through this baby, God saved us and repaired our relationship with him. Having been presented with such a great gift, we rejoice with the shepherds and angels.
As followers of Jesus, we cannot keep this news to ourselves. At Christmas, our rejoicing includes considering how we let others know of God's love.

......ON THE WAY TO MASS

How is it that little babies can claim an entire room? What do you notice about the way they interact with the world?

ON THE WAY HOME FROM MASS ......

Which person would you like to be in today's Gospel? Would you like to be the shepherds, angels, Mary, or Joseph?

Living the Word

Invite family members to choose a person in the story and share what they think that individual kept in his or her heart from this day. Then, ask family members to pick a different perspective and present their thoughts to the rest of the family as if they were in Bethlehem. What do they see, hear, smell, and think?

December 30, 2018

Feast of the Holy Family of Jesus, Mary, and Joseph

Hearing the Word

Luke 2:41–52

In the name of the Father, and of the Son, and of the Holy Spirit.

Each year Jesus' parents went to Jerusalem for the feast of Passover, and when he was twelve years old, they went up according to festival custom. After they had completed its days, as they were returning, the boy Jesus remained behind in Jerusalem, but his parents did not know it. Thinking he was in the caravan, they journeyed for a day and looked for him among their relatives and acquaintances, but not finding him, they returned to Jerusalem to look for him. After three days they found him in the temple, sitting in the midst of the teachers, listening to them and asking them questions, and all who heard him were astounded at his understanding and his answers. When his parents saw him, they were astonished, and his mother said to him, "Son, why have you done this to us? Your father and I have been looking for you with great anxiety." And he said to them, "Why were you looking for me? Did you not know that I must be in my Father's house?" But they did not understand what he said to them. He went down with them and came to Nazareth, and was obedient to them; and his mother kept all these things in her heart. And Jesus advanced in wisdom and age and favor before God and man.

Reflecting on the Word

Parents can identify with Mary and Joseph's concern and then be taken aback by Jesus' reply. This reading gives us a chance to consider the mysteries that are part of our lives. Jesus' statement did not give his parents an easy answer; it presented them with a mystery. Joseph and Mary went home with Jesus to live out the mystery. When we are confronted with what we do not understand, we need to hand ourselves over to live out the mystery.

•••••• ON THE WAY TO MASS

What would you have said to Jesus if you were his parent?

ON THE WAY HOME FROM MASS ••••••

Whom do you consider family?

Living the Word

Jesus shows us that our obligation extends beyond our immediate family to all of our brothers and sisters in Christ. Plan to take time to connect with your parish family. As a family, decide to attend an event, invite a new parish family over for dinner, or volunteer for a new ministry. See how bringing your small family into the bigger context of the parish family can grow both the church and your children's experiences.

SOLEMNITY OF MARY, THE HOLY MOTHER OF GOD

Hearing the Word

Luke 2:16–21

In the name of the Father, and of the Son, and of the Holy Spirit.

The shepherds went in haste to Bethlehem and found Mary and Joseph, and the infant lying in the manger. When they saw this, they made known the message that had been told them about this child. All who heard it were amazed by what had been told them by the shepherds. And Mary kept all these things, reflecting on them in her heart. Then the shepherds returned, glorifying and praising God for all they had heard and seen, just as it had been told to them.

When eight days were completed for his circumcision, he was named Jesus, the name given him by the angel before he was conceived in the womb.

Reflecting on the Word

Today's Gospel shows different responses to the birth of Jesus. The shepherds went quickly to Bethlehem to see the infant Jesus, told others of this good news, and then praised God. Mary, having given birth, reflected on the experience, pondering it in her heart. As we enter this new year, we should consider how we live out our response to the birth of Jesus. Do we spend time both reflecting on this birth and telling others what it means to us?

•••••• ON THE WAY TO MASS

What do you imagine the shepherds were thinking?

ON THE WAY HOME FROM MASS ••••••

What is something that would make this year great? What are you looking forward to?

Living the Word

As a family, dedicate this new year to the will of God. Family members may want to choose to put a blessing over a door in chalk, make individual resolutions, or decide on something or someone to dedicate their time, talent, or treasure to. Set markers on the calendar (or a reminder on your phone) every quarter to check back in to see how the family is progressing toward their goal and to periodically rededicate your lives to God's will.

January 6, 2019

Solemnity of the Epiphany of the Lord

Hearing the Word

Matthew 2:1–5, 7–12

In the name of the Father, and of the Son, and of the Holy Spirit.

When Jesus was born in Bethlehem of Judea, in the days of King Herod, behold, magi from the east arrived in Jerusalem, saying, "Where is the newborn king of the Jews? We saw his star at its rising and have come to do him homage." When King Herod heard this, he was greatly troubled, and all Jerusalem with him. Assembling all the chief priests and the scribes of the people, he inquired of them where the Christ was to be born. They said to him, "In Bethlehem of Judea . . ." Then Herod called the magi secretly and ascertained from them the time of the star's appearance. He sent them to Bethlehem and said, "Go and search diligently for the child. When you have found him, bring me word, that I too may go and do him homage." After their audience with the king they set out. And behold, the star that they had seen at its rising preceded them, until it came and stopped over the place where the child was. They were overjoyed at seeing the star, and on entering the house they saw the child with Mary his mother. They prostrated themselves and did him homage. Then they opened their treasures and offered him gifts of gold, frankincense, and myrrh. And having been warned in a dream not to return to Herod, they departed for their country by another way.

Reflecting on the Word

That a star announced Jesus' coming shows that God holds all of the universe in care and love. As we celebrate that God sent Jesus to people of all nations, we will want to remember that creation is to be respected and honored. Pope Francis' encyclical *Laudato Si'* calls for humankind to examine how the planet is treated. Each of us will want to consider how we treat the signs and wonders God has given us.

•••••• ON THE WAY TO MASS

If you could choose a sign to announce your birth, what would it be?

ON THE WAY HOME FROM MASS ••••••

What gift(s) would you want to bring Jesus, Mary, and Joseph if Christ were born today?

Living the Word

On this celebration of the Epiphany, gift each other with a service, experience, or something else that is not a material good. The gifts of the Magi were symbolic. What could each person in the family do for others that would carry significance?

January 13, 2019

Feast of the Baptism of the Lord

Hearing the Word

Luke 3:15–16, 21–22

In the name of the Father, and of the Son, and of the Holy Spirit.

The people were filled with expectation, and all were asking in their hearts whether John might be the Christ. John answered them all, saying, "I am baptizing you with water; but one mightier than I is coming. I am not worthy to stoop and loosen the thongs of his sandals. He will baptize you with the Holy Spirit and fire."

After all the people had been baptized and Jesus also had been baptized and was praying, heaven was opened and the Holy Spirit descended upon him in a bodily form like a dove. And a voice came from heaven, "You are my beloved Son; with you I am well pleased."

Reflecting on the Word

Parents, grandparents, and other family members anticipate the Baptism of a child with joy. Through the sacrament, the baby becomes an adopted child of God. This is a special time when the true holiness of an individual is illuminated in the light of the Holy Spirit. Bathed in the baptismal waters, we enter the Church. With the support of the faith community, the relationship of the Christian is nurtured and the individual brings the light of Christ to the world.

•••••• ON THE WAY TO MASS

Tell your children something about the day of their Baptism.

ON THE WAY HOME FROM MASS ••••••

In this reading, the Holy Spirit appeared as a dove. What form might the Holy Spirit take today?

Living the Word

The Holy Spirit is among us, adding richness to our lives. With your family, walk around your neighborhood and see what blessings and marvels you witness. Record what you notice. Where do you see the Holy Spirit active and engaged today? What kinds of things do you notice that inspire or challenge you? What can each family member learn from the perspective of the others?

January 20, 2019

Second Sunday in Ordinary Time

Hearing the Word

John 2:1–11

In the name of the Father, and of the Son, and of the Holy Spirit.

There was a wedding at Cana in Galilee, and the mother of Jesus was there. Jesus and his disciples were also invited to the wedding. When the wine ran short, the mother of Jesus said to him, "They have no wine." And Jesus said to her, "Woman, how does your concern affect me? My hour has not yet come." His mother said to the servers, "Do whatever he tells you." Now there were six stone water jars there for Jewish ceremonial washings, each holding twenty to thirty gallons. Jesus told them, "Fill the jars with water." So they filled them to the brim. Then he told them, "Draw some out now and take it to the headwaiter." So they took it. And when the headwaiter tasted the water that had become wine, without knowing where it came from—although the servers who had drawn the water knew—, the headwaiter called the bridegroom and said to him, "Everyone serves good wine first, and then when people have drunk freely, an inferior one; but you have kept the good wine until now." Jesus did this as the beginning of his signs at Cana in Galilee and so revealed his glory, and his disciples began to believe in him.

Reflecting on the Word

In today's Gospel, we see Mary summon Jesus to solve a dilemma at a wedding feast. Mary is, in effect, calling Jesus to start his ministry. When Jesus turns the water into wine, Jesus is not only solving what seems to be a problem but beginning the work for which his Father sent him. His hour had come. Sometimes we do not realize that we are being called to do the work of God. We must always be open to the mystery of being called and allow God to transform us for the work we must do.

•••••• ON THE WAY TO MASS

What can you give to the world? What might happen if you do so?

ON THE WAY HOME FROM MASS ••••••

How can you encourage another to follow the will of God?

Living the Word

Give each family member water in a see-through cup and some red food coloring. Ask family members to name the kind acts they have seen each other perform. As each person names these kindnesses, add a drop of food coloring to the water. With every act of naming, see how much more the water changes. Noticing someone's spark can help that spark grow. When you are finished, drink up and celebrate the uniqueness that is each person.

January 27, 2019

Third Sunday in Ordinary Time

Hearing the Word

Luke 4:14–21

In the name of the Father, and of the Son, and of the Holy Spirit.

Jesus returned to Galilee in the power of the Spirit, and news of him spread throughout the whole region. He taught in their synagogues and was praised by all.

He came to Nazareth, where he had grown up, and went according to his custom into the synagogue on the sabbath day. He stood up to read and was handed a scroll of the prophet Isaiah. He unrolled the scroll and found the passage where it was written: / *The Spirit of the Lord is upon me, / because he has anointed me / to bring glad tidings to the poor. / He has sent me to proclaim liberty to captives / and recovery of sight to the blind, / to let the oppressed go free, / and to proclaim a year acceptable to the Lord.* / Rolling up the scroll, he handed it back to the attendant and sat down, and the eyes of all in the synagogue looked intently at him. He said to them, "Today this Scripture passage is fulfilled in your hearing."

Reflecting on the Word

After proclaiming the passage from Isaiah, Jesus announces that he is the one the prophet had foretold. Can you imagine the response of his hearers? Do you think that they had a hard time believing the messiah was in their midst? Would they want to wait for another to come? Have there been times that it is hard to believe that God is in your midst?

. . . . . . ON THE WAY TO MASS

What promise are you waiting to have fulfilled? What would you do if it came to be?

ON THE WAY HOME FROM MASS . . . . . .

How could you bring glad tidings to another?

Living the Word

God is fulfilling a promise through each of our lives. As a family, write a mission statement or promise to God. What is God fulfilling through your family? What promise does your family want to make to God in return for the gifts that you have been given? Your family statement might be written in a few sentences or in the form of a poem or a drawing.

February 3, 2019

FOURTH SUNDAY IN ORDINARY TIME

Hearing the Word

Luke 4:21–30

In the name of the Father, and of the Son, and of the Holy Spirit.

Jesus began speaking in the synagogue, saying: "Today this Scripture passage is fulfilled in your hearing." And all spoke highly of him and were amazed at the gracious words that came from his mouth. They also asked, "Isn't this the son of Joseph?" He said to them, "Surely you will quote me this proverb, 'Physician, cure yourself,' and say, 'Do here in your native place the things that we heard were done in Capernaum.'" And he said, "Amen, I say to you, no prophet is accepted in his own native place. Indeed, I tell you, there were many widows in Israel in the days of Elijah when the sky was closed for three and a half years and a severe famine spread over the entire land. It was to none of these that Elijah was sent, but only to a widow in Zarephath in the land of Sidon. Again, there were many lepers in Israel during the time of Elisha the prophet; yet not one of them was cleansed, but only Naaman the Syrian." When the people in the synagogue heard this, they were all filled with fury. They rose up, drove him out of the town, and led him to the brow of the hill on which their town had been built, to hurl him down headlong. But Jesus passed through the midst of them and went away.

Reflecting on the Word

Jesus is back in his hometown among friends and family and yet they cannot hear him. All they see is the small boy they knew. Too often we let what we are so sure of get in the way of the reality we face. It is important to be open to seeing people and events in new ways. When we fail to do that, we may miss the presence of God among us.

•••••• ON THE WAY TO MASS

What is a thought or idea that has challenged you in the last few weeks? Why was it so hard?

ON THE WAY HOME FROM MASS ••••••

When was something so familiar that you disregarded its importance?

Living the Word

Ask family members to take turns naming something about each other that they are sure is true. When a statement is made about an individual, that person gets a chance to respond to the perception. Be sure to direct that only positive comments can be made. A child might say, for instance, that they know that their father is careful to call his mother each week. After the exercise, ask family members what it is like to be seen through another's eyes and if they learned more about each other. Finally, ask each person to name something about themselves that they think no one else realizes.

February 10, 2019

Fifth Sunday in Ordinary Time

Hearing the Word

Luke 5:4–11

In the name of the Father, and of the Son, and of the Holy Spirit.

[Jesus] said to Simon, "Put out into deep water and lower your nets for a catch." Simon said in reply, "Master, we have worked hard all night and have caught nothing, but at your command I will lower the nets." When they had done this, they caught a great number of fish and their nets were tearing. They signaled to their partners in the other boat to come to help them. They came and filled both boats so that the boats were in danger of sinking. When Simon Peter saw this, he fell at the knees of Jesus and said, "Depart from me, Lord, for I am a sinful man." For astonishment at the catch of fish they had made seized him and all those with him, and likewise James and John, the sons of Zebedee, who were partners of Simon. Jesus said to Simon, "Do not be afraid; from now on you will be catching men." When they brought their boats to the shore, they left everything and followed him.

Reflecting on the Word

Many times Jesus cautions his followers not to be afraid. Through Jesus, the disciples experienced many things out of the ordinary, so some apprehension would be natural. Jesus, however, counsels them to trust. Sometimes we are presented with situations that seem to call forth strength and courage from us. In today's Gospel, we see that we are not to rely on such attributes; we are only to rely on God. Jesus shows the disciples that he can fill their nets only for Peter to declare that he is unworthy. Jesus calls us as we are and asks that we put our trust in him.

......ON THE WAY TO MASS

What have you missed because of fear? What would you have done differently?

ON THE WAY HOME FROM MASS ......

Would you have stayed in the boat with Jesus?

Living the Word

The correct tools are needed to catch fish and people. Ask your family to brainstorm to make a list of what is needed to fish. (Hint: a line, hooks, bobbers, sinkers, worms, lures, needle-nose pliers, first aid kit, sunscreen, line cutter, a boat, and a fishing hat are among the items.) Discuss how the fish will get away if you do not have the essentials. Then ask the family what is needed to bring people to the Lord. These items may not be as tangible as what fishers need. Love, patience, and kindness will be among what is required.

February 17, 2019

Sixth Sunday in Ordinary Time

Hearing the Word

Luke 6:17, 20–23

In the name of the Father, and of the Son, and of the Holy Spirit.

Jesus came down with the Twelve and stood on a stretch of level ground . . . And raising his eyes toward his disciples he said: / "Blessed are you who are poor, / for the kingdom of God is yours. / Blessed are you who are now hungry, / for you will be satisfied. / Blessed are you who are now weeping, / for you will laugh. / Blessed are you when people hate you, / and when they exclude and insult you, / and denounce your name as evil / on account of the Son of Man. / Rejoice and leap for joy on that day! Behold, your reward will be great in heaven."

Reflecting on the Word

In God's time all things are fleeting. We look forward to the day when our poverty will be replaced with the Kingdom of God. Though today we may cry over a loss, one day we will experience wholeness in God. Jesus shows the people that their tears, suffering, and faithfulness to the Lord are not forgotten. They may not receive accolades in this life, but God will rejoice with them for all eternity.

·······ON THE WAY TO MASS

When have you felt blessed? Have you ever felt blessed during a sad experience?

ON THE WAY HOME FROM MASS ·······

Which Beatitude do you most easily identify with? Why?

Living the Word

Ask each family member to make a list of their blessings. Those who feel artistic could draw their blessings. Write down a master list of the blessings and then make a paper chain of the blessings, with one blessing per link on the chain. String this up as a reminder of all the good things for which the family is thankful. When someone is feeling down, detach one of the chains and read it as a reminder. Once the chain is completely dismantled, the process can be started all over again.

February 24, 2019

Seventh Sunday in Ordinary Time

Hearing the Word

Luke 6:27–38

In the name of the Father, and of the Son, and of the Holy Spirit.

Jesus said to his disciples: "To you who hear I say, love your enemies, do good to those who hate you, bless those who curse you, pray for those who mistreat you. To the person who strikes you on one cheek, offer the other one as well, and from the person who takes your cloak, do not withhold even your tunic. Give to everyone who asks of you, and from the one who takes what is yours do not demand it back. Do to others as you would have them do to you. For if you love those who love you, what credit is that to you? Even sinners love those who love them. And if you do good to those who do good to you, what credit is that to you? Even sinners do the same. If you lend money to those from whom you expect repayment, what credit is that to you? Even sinners lend to sinners, and get back the same amount. But rather, love your enemies and do good to them, and lend expecting nothing back; then your reward will be great and you will be children of the Most High, for he himself is kind to the ungrateful and the wicked. Be merciful, just as your Father is merciful."

Reflecting on the Word

To be a Christian is to go above and beyond the basics. Since we know and hold the light of God in our lives, we are required to do so much more than those who do not know Christ. We have not only the grace to be able to do more but also the responsibility. No matter how hard it is to pray for someone who has harmed us, we must still do so. Such acts soften our hearts and allow grace to fill us. When we open ourselves to follow Christ, the Holy Spirit can work within us.

...... ON THE WAY TO MASS

Who or what could use more love in your life?

ON THE WAY HOME FROM MASS ......

What is something nice you did for someone else without expecting anything in return?

Living the Word

Through role-playing, help your family find ways to love others when it is difficult. Encourage each family member to be on both sides of a scenario in which one person is rude and the other acts in a loving way. As a family, brainstorm different things the loving person could say or various ways they could react to the difficult situation. Come up with some specific phrases that would be helpful to have on hand when trying to love those who are being hurtful.

March 3, 2019

Eighth Sunday in Ordinary Time

Hearing the Word

Luke 6:39–45

In the name of the Father, and of the Son, and of the Holy Spirit.

Jesus told his disciples a parable, "Can a blind person guide a blind person? Will not both fall into a pit? No disciple is superior to the teacher; but when fully trained, every disciple will be like his teacher. Why do you notice the splinter in your brother's eye, but do not perceive the wooden beam in your own? How can you say to your brother, 'Brother, let me remove that splinter in your eye,' when you do not even notice the wooden beam in your own eye? You hypocrite! Remove the wooden beam from your eye first; then you will see clearly to remove the splinter in your brother's eye.

"A good tree does not bear rotten fruit, nor does a rotten tree bear good fruit. For every tree is known by its own fruit. For people do not pick figs from thorn bushes, nor do they gather grapes from brambles. A good person out of the store of goodness in his heart produces good, but an evil person out of a store of evil produces evil; for from the fullness of the heart the mouth speaks."

Reflecting on the Word

"A good tree does not bear rotten fruit, nor does a rotten tree bear good fruit." Each day we build up habits and attitudes that either orient us toward God or away from that love. When an individual uses opportunities to do good, virtue is fostered. Even when the gestures of goodness are small ones, the person is increasingly conforming to the image of God. As we prioritize what is important in our lives, we want to remember that we will be known by our fruits.

......ON THE WAY TO MASS

What is one thing you would like to change about your daily interactions?

ON THE WAY HOME FROM MASS ......

How can you be more aware of what may be standing in the way of seeing clearly?

Living the Word

Play a memory game with the family. Gather some objects and lay them out on the table under a covered cloth. As you uncover the items briefly, let everyone look at them for the first time. Then, cover them up and ask the family to write down the things they remember seeing. Discuss whether additional time or working together would aid memory. What faults act like the cover and make it hard for us to see things clearly? How can we remove these obstacles?

March 10, 2019

First Sunday of Lent

Hearing the Word
Luke 4:1–13

In the name of the Father, and of the Son, and of the Holy Spirit.

Filled with the Holy Spirit, Jesus returned from the Jordan
and was led by the Spirit into the desert for forty days, to
be tempted by the devil. He ate nothing during those days,
and when they were over he was hungry. The devil said to
him, "If you are the Son of God, command this stone to
become bread." Jesus answered him, "It is written, *One
does not live on bread alone.*" Then he took him up and
showed him all the kingdoms of the world in a single
instant. The devil said to him, "I shall give to you all this
power and glory; for it has been handed over to me, and I
may give it to whomever I wish. All this will be yours, if
you worship me." Jesus said to him in reply, "It is written: /
*You shall worship the Lord, your God, / and him alone shall
you serve.*" / Then he led him to Jerusalem, made him
stand on the parapet of the temple, and said to him, "If you
are the Son of God, throw yourself down from here, for it is
written: / *He will command his angels concerning you, to
guard you, / and: / With their hands they will support you, /
lest you dash your foot against a stone.*" / Jesus said to him
in reply, "It also says, *You shall not put the Lord, your God,
to the test.*" When the devil had finished every temptation,
he departed from him for a time.

Reflecting on the Word

The devil tempts Jesus to serve himself. Jesus could feed himself, possess all power, and have the angels come to aid him. But Jesus knew who he was and that he did not come to this earth to serve himself. Any power that Jesus uses reveals the glory of God. It is easy to fall for the temptation to serve ourselves instead of God. During this Lent, we may want to examine what tempts us to be a replacement for God. How do you keep your eyes focused on worshipping God alone?

● ● ● ● ● ● ON THE WAY TO MASS

Describe something or someone that is hard for you to say no to even if you should. Why?

ON THE WAY HOME FROM MASS ● ● ● ● ● ●

Do you know who you are? How does this help you resist temptations?

Living the Word

Lent is a time to explore our relationship with God. At the heart of that relationship is knowledge of ourselves as children of God. During the next few weeks, take your family on a journey of self-exploration. To begin, invite all of them to draw a portrait that shows how they see themselves. When the portraits are finished, invite each person to talk about his or her work. Place the drawings prominently in the home.

March 17, 2019

Second Sunday of Lent

Hearing the Word

Luke 9:28b–36

In the name of the Father, and of the Son, and of the Holy Spirit.

Jesus took Peter, John, and James and went up the mountain to pray. While he was praying his face changed in appearance and his clothing became dazzling white. And behold, two men were conversing with him, Moses and Elijah, who appeared in glory and spoke of his exodus that he was going to accomplish in Jerusalem. Peter and his companions had been overcome by sleep, but becoming fully awake, they saw his glory and the two men standing with him. As they were about to part from him, Peter said to Jesus, "Master, it is good that we are here; let us make three tents, one for you, one for Moses, and one for Elijah." But he did not know what he was saying. While he was still speaking, a cloud came and cast a shadow over them, and they became frightened when they entered the cloud. Then from the cloud came a voice that said, "This is my chosen Son; listen to him." After the voice had spoken, Jesus was found alone. They fell silent and did not at that time tell anyone what they had seen.

Reflecting on the Word

At the Transfiguration, the three Apostles are allowed to view Jesus in his divinity. They knew Jesus as human, and now they have a glimpse of his divine nature. In this instance, Peter, James, and John are allowed another perspective of Jesus. During Lent, we will not enter a cloud as the Apostles did, but we can give ourselves a chance to see ourselves, one another, and creation with different eyes. If you could see how you and those around you are made in the image of God, what would you see?

......ON THE WAY TO MASS

What might God's vision reveal in you?

ON THE WAY HOME FROM MASS ......

Moses and Elijah stand with Jesus in today's Gospel. Who inspires and stands with you?

Living the Word

We never stand alone in our journey. Last week each person created a self-portrait, but our true identity also contains the visions of us that others hold. Ask each family member to add to the portraits of each person, showing the family members as God sees them. Words, phrases, images, or simply more color or background can be added. Encourage the family to give each picture context and depth. Take a moment to explore these family collages and notice the fuller picture they now represent.

Third Sunday of Lent

Hearing the Word

Luke 13:1–9

In the name of the Father, and of the Son, and of the Holy Spirit.

Some people told Jesus about the Galileans whose blood Pilate had mingled with the blood of their sacrifices. Jesus said to them in reply, "Do you think that because these Galileans suffered in this way they were greater sinners than all other Galileans? By no means! But I tell you, if you do not repent, you will all perish as they did! Or those eighteen people who were killed when the tower at Siloam fell on them—do you think they were more guilty than everyone else who lived in Jerusalem? By no means! But I tell you, if you do not repent, you will all perish as they did!"

And he told them this parable: "There once was a person who had a fig tree planted in his orchard, and when he came in search of fruit on it but found none, he said to the gardener, 'For three years now I have come in search of fruit on this fig tree but have found none. So cut it down. Why should it exhaust the soil?' He said to him in reply, 'Sir, leave it for this year also, and I shall cultivate the ground around it and fertilize it; it may bear fruit in the future. If not you can cut it down.'"

Reflecting on the Word

Jesus calls the people to turn their lives to God or risk perishing just as those whose deaths they decry. With the parable of the fig tree, Jesus shows his inquisitors that it is possible to turn their lives around, even if they have not borne good fruit in years. Just as the gardener will seek to nourish the fig tree through cultivating the ground and fertilizer, we can nurture our relationship with God through prayer and good works.

•••••• ON THE WAY TO MASS

What does it mean to be guilty? When was a time you felt guilty?

ON THE WAY HOME FROM MASS ••••••

What would you like to repent of during this Lenten season?

Living the Word

Part of who we are includes our faults and mistakes. Ask each person to add a red ribbon or red color to their portrait to symbolize their flaws and weaknesses. Then encourage each family member to ask the rest of the family for forgiveness for one of these failings. Discuss how the family will help each person try to overcome a shortcoming.

Fourth Sunday of Lent

Hearing the Word

Luke 15:11a, 13b, 14a, 14c, 20a, 20f–22a,
23b–24, 25, 28, 29, 31–32

In the name of the Father, and of the Son, and of the Holy Spirit.

[Jesus said]: "A man had two sons, . . . the younger son collected all his belongings and set off to a distant country where he squandered his inheritance on a life of dissipation. When he had freely spent everything, . . . he found himself in dire need. . . . Coming to his senses, . . . he got up and went back to his father. While he was still a long way off, his father . . . ran to his son, embraced him and kissed him. His son said to him, 'Father, I have sinned against heaven and against you; I no longer deserve to be called your son.' But his father ordered his servants, . . . 'Let us celebrate with a feast, because this son of mine was dead, and has come to life again; he was lost, and has been found.' Then the celebration began. Now the older son had been out in the field and, on his way back, as he neared the house, he heard the sound of music and dancing. . . . He became angry, and when he refused to enter the house, his father came out and pleaded with him. He said to his father in reply, 'Look, all these years I served you and not once did I disobey your orders; yet you never gave me even a young goat to feast on with my friends. . . . [His father] said to him, 'My son you are here with me always; everything I have is yours. But now we must celebrate and rejoice, because your brother was dead and has come to life again; he was lost and has been found.'"

Reflecting on the Word

No matter our sin and no matter how long we have been away from God, our return is celebrated. In this parable, Jesus portrays God as a father who not only waits for the son but runs to meet him. Such is the father's joy that he embraces and kisses his son before receiving an apology. We, too, can always return to God after we have fallen away from the path and neglected our relationship with God. Our Lord is always waiting for us.

· · · · · · ON THE WAY TO MASS

Have you ever felt lost? What was it like?

ON THE WAY HOME FROM MASS · · · · · ·

Have you ever felt the love of acceptance even when you were less than your best self?

Living the Word

Explain to the family that sometimes we can be physically close to someone but still need to return to them. Ask your family to take time to consider what has been lost in their lives. Perhaps someone has lost joy in simple things. Another person might have lost the ability to see the gift that even a younger sibling can be. Have a coming home celebration for these things. Ask your family members to add a physical object to sit near their portrait to symbolize what is making a return in their life.

Fifth Sunday of Lent

Hearing the Word

John 8:3–11

In the name of the Father, and of the Son, and of the Holy Spirit.

The scribes and the Pharisees brought a woman who had been caught in adultery and made her stand in the middle. They said to him, "Teacher, this woman was caught in the very act of committing adultery. Now in the law, Moses commanded us to stone such women. So what do you say?" They said this to test him, so that they could have some charge to bring against him. Jesus bent down and began to write on the ground with his finger. But when they continued asking him, he straightened up and said to them, "Let the one among you who is without sin be the first to throw a stone at her." Again he bent down and wrote on the ground. And in response, they went away one by one, beginning with the elders. So he was left alone with the woman before him. Then Jesus straightened up and said to her, "Woman, where are they? Has no one condemned you?" She replied, "No one, sir." Then Jesus said, "Neither do I condemn you. Go, and from now on do not sin any more."

Reflecting on the Word

We hear of condemnation in the news, at school, and at work. Often, we have no trouble handing out judgments and may be hardest on ourselves. Perhaps that's why we are quick to throw stones at others. When we are alarmed by a weakness or imperfection in another, we might want to consider how that defect is manifested in our lives. Instead of concentrating on the wrong, we can seek to identify with the person and become a companion in compassion.

•••••• ON THE WAY TO MASS

When have you criticized another? What part of the person reminded you of yourself?

ON THE WAY HOME FROM MASS ••••••

How can we help those who have gone astray?

Living the Word

Add stones to your portrait area today. Instead of stones of condemnation, celebrate your strengths and what makes you able to be foundations for the Kingdom of God. Take time to choose stones you find outside or from a special collection. Let each person name the strength that each stone represents. Jesus chose to build others up instead of tearing them down. Let us do the same as we come closer to celebrating Easter.

April 14, 2019

Palm Sunday of the Passion of the Lord

Hearing the Word

Luke 19:36–40

In the name of the Father, and of the Son, and of the Holy Spirit.

As [Jesus] rode along, the people were spreading their cloaks on the road; and now as he was approaching the slope of the Mount of Olives, the whole multitude of his disciples began to praise God aloud with joy for all the mighty deeds they had seen. They proclaimed: / "Blessed is the king who comes / in the name of the Lord. / Peace in heaven / and glory in the highest." / Some of the Pharisees in the crowd said to him, "Teacher, rebuke your disciples." He said in reply, "I tell you, if they keep silent, the stones will cry out!"

Reflecting on the Word

As we take our palm branches before the procession today, we enter into the holiest of weeks in the liturgical year. Palm Sunday begins with our joining with the disciples of Jesus' time in rejoicing that the Messiah has come. The Gospel at the procession is clear that even creation knows that Jesus should be praised. When the Pharisees told Jesus to rebuke his disciples, we hear that if the followers do not praise Jesus, then the stones will do so.

......ON THE WAY TO MASS

What did it mean to you to carry the palm branch last year?

ON THE WAY HOME FROM MASS ......

Why do we rejoice today even before Jesus rises from the dead?

Living the Word

In the main Gospel today we heard Jesus wrongfully accused. Our identity exists in community and is reflected in the way we treat each other. If my brother or sister suffers, so do I. Read aloud to your family a true story about a wrongfully accused prisoner who will finally be exonerated. As a family, write this person a letter. See what you can find out about the person's life and share as much as is age-appropriate. If possible, send the letter to the person. Add the person's portrait to those of the family and hold them in prayer.

Easter Sunday of the Resurrection of the Lord

Hearing the Word

John 20:1–9

In the name of the Father, and of the Son, and of the Holy Spirit.

On the first day of the week, Mary of Magdala came to the tomb early in the morning, while it was still dark, and saw the stone removed from the tomb. So she ran and went to Simon Peter and to the other disciple whom Jesus loved, and told them, "They have taken the Lord from the tomb, and we don't know where they put him." So Peter and the other disciple went out and came to the tomb. They both ran, but the other disciple ran faster than Peter and arrived at the tomb first; he bent down and saw the burial cloths there, but did not go in. When Simon Peter arrived after him, he went into the tomb and saw the burial cloths there, and the cloth that had covered his head, not with the burial cloths but rolled up in a separate place. Then the other disciple also went in, the one who had arrived at the tomb first, and he saw and believed. For they did not yet understand the Scripture that he had to rise from the dead.

Reflecting on the Word

Since we celebrate the reality of Jesus' Resurrection every Sunday, it is hard for us to imagine how shocking this event must have been for Mary and the disciples. However, they did not need to fully understand the mystery to experience and spread the joy. Neither do we. We don't have to be theologians or scholars to spread the Good News of Easter. If we truly let the joy of the Resurrection fill our hearts, we can't help but tell those we love about it.

• • • • • • ON THE WAY TO MASS

Is there anyone you would like to tell about Jesus' Resurrection? What is stopping you?

ON THE WAY HOME FROM MASS • • • • • •

What is a reason you have to exclaim "alleluia" in your life?

Living the Word

This is the final week with your Lenten portraits. Decorate and exult them along with the journey they have taken you on. Perhaps add ribbons, stickers, or glitter. Ask each person to take time to reflect on how he or she has changed. Invite the family to explore the questions: Would you draw your picture the same way? What have you learned about yourself? Family members can take their picture and keep it in their room as a reminder of their growth.

April 28, 2019

Second Sunday of Easter / Sunday of Divine Mercy

Hearing the Word

John 20:19–29

In the name of the Father, and of the Son, and of the Holy Spirit.

On the evening of that first day of the week, when the doors were locked, where the disciples were, . . . Jesus came and stood in their midst and said to them, "Peace be with you." When he had said this, he showed them his hands and his side. The disciples rejoiced when they saw the Lord. Jesus said to them again, "Peace be with you. As the Father has sent me, so I send you." And when he had said this, he breathed on them and said to them, "Receive the Holy Spirit. Whose sins you forgive are forgiven them, and whose sins you retain are retained."

Thomas, called Didymus, one of the Twelve, was not with them when Jesus came. So the other disciples said to him, "We have seen the Lord." But he said to them, "Unless I see the mark of the nails in his hands and put my finger into the nailmarks and put my hand into his side, I will not believe."

Now a week later . . . Jesus came . . . and said, "Peace be with you." Then he said to Thomas, "Put your finger here and see my hands, and bring your hand and put it into my side, and do not be unbelieving, but believe." Thomas answered and said to him, "My Lord and my God!" Jesus said to him, "Have you come to believe because you have seen me? Blessed are those who have not seen and have believed."

Reflecting on the Word

Jesus emphasizes the gift of peace as he comes in peace and sends the disciples out in peace. This reminds us that he is the Prince of Peace (Isaiah 9:5). Jesus exercises power for peace. He comes in peace, with peace, and for peace. His message remains consistent and pure as he avoids violence of any kind.

• • • • • • ON THE WAY TO MASS

Why does Jesus emphasize peace?

ON THE WAY HOME FROM MASS • • • • • •

The Second Sunday of Easter also is called the Sunday of Divine Mercy. How are peace and mercy related?

Living the Word

Just as Thomas doubted, so do we at times. Ask each person to make a list of doubts or worries and then rate them from one to five, with one being very important and five the least urgent. Go through the lists as a family and see if sharing doubts eases the burden. Is there another way family members can help share the burden? After the discussion, invite the family to look at the lists again. Would they rate anything differently now?

May 5, 2019

Third Sunday of Easter

Hearing the Word

John 21:1–9, 12, 15–17

In the name of the Father, and of the Son, and of the Holy Spirit.

At that time, Jesus revealed himself again to his disciples . . .
Together were Simon Peter, Thomas called Didymus, Nath
anael . . . Zebedee's sons, and two others of his disciples.
Simon Peter said to them, "I am going fishing." They said
to him, "We also will come with you." . . . When it was
already dawn, Jesus was standing on the shore; . . .
"Children, have you caught anything to eat?" They answered
him, "No." So he said to them, "Cast the net over the right
side of the boat and you will find something." So they cast
it, and were not able to pull it in because of the number
of fish. So the disciple whom Jesus loved said to Peter,
"It is the Lord." When Simon Peter heard that it was the
Lord, . . . he jumped into the sea. The other disciples
came in the boat . . . dragging the net with the fish.
When they climbed out on shore, . . . Jesus said to
them, "Come, have breakfast." . . .

When they had finished breakfast, Jesus said to Simon
Peter, "Simon, son of John, do you love me more than
these?" Simon Peter answered him, "Yes, Lord, you know
that I love you." Jesus said to him, "Feed my lambs." He
then said to Simon Peter a second time, "Simon, son of
John, do you love me?" Simon Peter answered him, "Yes,
Lord, you know that I love you." Jesus said to him, "Tend

my sheep." Jesus said to him the third time, "Simon, son of John, do you love me?" Peter was distressed that Jesus had said to him a third time, "Do you love me?" and he said to him, "Lord you know everything; you know that I love you." Jesus said to him, "Feed my sheep."

Reflecting on the Word

The bounty of this catch of fish portrays that God will provide disciples with what is needed as they go out to feed the people. How often do we withhold the nourishment of time, attention, and affection, pleading that we barely have enough to feed ourselves? As we nurture others, we rely on the abundance that God gives.

......ON THE WAY TO MASS

Whom can you nourish this week with your time and attention?

ON THE WAY HOME FROM MASS ......

Who are the "sheep" Jesus refers to?

Living the Word

Invite some friends to a feast filled with what nourishes all of you. The feast could include a mixture of storytelling, art, poetry, and music. Make sure that each person is interested in at least some of what will be offered. Be sure, too, that all know this is a screen-free time.

May 12, 2019

Fourth Sunday of Easter

Hearing the Word

John 10:27–30

In the name of the Father, and of the Son, and of the Holy Spirit.

Jesus said, "My sheep hear my voice; I know them, and they follow me. I give them eternal life, and they shall never perish. No one can take them out of my hand. My Father, who has given them to me, is greater than all, and no one can take them out of the Father's hand. The Father and I are one."

Reflecting on the Word

The sheep know Jesus' voice because they have formed a relationship with him during the time they have spent together. This Gospel may prompt an examination of our relationship with God. As time is spent with God in prayer, a relationship will be nurtured and it will be easier to distinguish God's voice from another's. If we do not spend time with God in prayer, we may heed the wrong call and stray from the one who loves us.

......ON THE WAY TO MASS

Did you ever think you knew exactly where you were going and still ended up lost? What was that like?

ON THE WAY HOME FROM MASS ......

How does God help and protect us as a shepherd would?

Living the Word

Lead the family in playing "shepherd and sheep" or hide-and-seek with a twist. The person who is the shepherd is "it," while everyone else plays the sheep. While staying in one spot, the shepherd counts with open eyes, trying to keep track of everyone as they hide. Once done counting, the shepherd rounds up the sheep. As each person takes a turn as a shepherd, participants should keep track of who is the fastest at rounding up the sheep. After the game is over, ask family members what kind of skills it takes to keep track of everyone and how hard it was to do so.

May 19, 2019

Fifth Sunday of Easter

Hearing the Word

John 13:31–33a, 34–35

In the name of the Father, and of the Son, and of the Holy Spirit.

When Judas had left them, Jesus said, "Now is the Son of Man glorified, and God is glorified in him. If God is glorified in him, God will also glorify him in himself, and God will glorify him at once. My children, I will be with you only a little while longer. I give you a new commandment: love one another. As I have loved you, so you also should love one another. This is how all will know that you are my disciples, if you have love for one another."

Reflecting on the Word

Loving each other as God loves us is a steep command. With such love comes forgiveness, mercy, and compassion. We might ask ourselves how we can love each person as God loves. Though we certainly fall short of loving as God does, we are to strive to love others perfectly. Every day we are presented with multiple opportunities to love as God would have us. It is up to us to seek to accept this challenge each time.

......ON THE WAY TO MASS

Who in your life do you feel loves and sees you as God does?

ON THE WAY HOME FROM MASS ......

In what ways do you show God's love to others in words, gifts, and actions?

Living the Word

Ask each family member to cut out about a dozen little hearts and write different ways they can show God's love to one another on each little heart and sign them. Hide these hearts around the house for people to find in a book they are reading, in their bed, or another place, or surprise them in their lunch. When a heart is found, the finder brings it to its author. When presented with a heart, the author must do what is noted. The hearts can be hidden again or their number may be increased.

May 26, 2019

Sixth Sunday of Easter

Hearing the Word

John 14:23–29

In the name of the Father, and of the Son, and of the Holy Spirit.

Jesus said to his disciples: "Whoever loves me will keep my word, and my Father will love him, and we will come to him and make our dwelling with him. Whoever does not love me does not keep my words; yet the word you hear is not mine but that of the Father who sent me.

"I have told you this while I am with you. The Advocate, the Holy Spirit whom the Father will send in my name, will teach you everything and remind you of all that I told you. Peace I leave with you; my peace I give to you. Not as the world gives do I give it to you. Do not let your hearts be troubled or afraid. You heard me tell you, 'I am going away and I will come back to you.' If you loved me, you would rejoice that I am going to the Father; for the Father is greater than I. And now I have told you this before it happens, so that when it happens you may believe."

Reflecting on the Word

As Jesus prepares his followers for his leaving, he tells them that they will not be alone. Not only will the Father and Jesus come to those who keep his word, but also the Holy Spirit will teach and remind them of what Jesus told them while on earth. Jesus assures these disciples that the peace he gives them will continue to be theirs. Finally, he assures them that he will return. Are you able to turn your anxieties over to God?

• • • • • • ON THE WAY TO MASS

What does it mean to keep God's Word? How do you do that?

ON THE WAY HOME FROM MASS • • • • • •

What qualities make something a home? What does it mean to be home?

Living the Word

With your family, create a dream dwelling. Fill it with qualities and memories instead of things. Draw your house plans together on a large piece of paper, and in each room, write the experiences and qualities you want to occur and feel there. For example, in the bedroom you could write "sweet dreams" and in the kitchen, "hospitality." In this drawing, you may also include the people you want to feel welcome in your home.

June 2, 2019

SOLEMNITY OF THE ASCENSION OF THE LORD

Hearing the Word

Luke 24:46–53

In the name of the Father, and of the Son, and of the Holy Spirit.

Jesus said to his disciples: "Thus it is written that the Christ would suffer and rise from the dead on the third day and that repentance, for the forgiveness of sins, would be preached in his name to all the nations, beginning from Jerusalem. You are witnesses of these things. And behold I am sending the promise of my Father upon you; but stay in the city until you are clothed with power from on high."

Then he led them out as far as Bethany, raised his hands, and blessed them. As he blessed them he parted from them and was taken up to heaven. They did him homage and then returned to Jerusalem with great joy, and they were continually in the temple praising God.

Reflecting on the Word

Surely, the disciples watched with conflicted hearts as Jesus was taken up into heaven. It must have been hard to see Jesus leave, and yet the Gospel states that the disciples returned to Jerusalem "with great joy." Today's reading from Acts tells of an angel urging the disciples to move on as they watched as Jesus left them. That angel helped them see that they needed to be about the mission that Jesus left to them. An entire world needed to hear about the Good News of Christ's life, death, and Resurrection.

•••••• ON THE WAY TO MASS

Have you ever just wanted to hold onto a moment and make it last forever? Why do things always need to move ahead?

ON THE WAY HOME FROM MASS ••••••

Have you ever had a friend move away? Was it hard to say good-bye? How did you keep in touch?

Living the Word

Gather your family to find examples in the Bible of Jesus appearing after his Resurrection. With a long roll of paper, help the family make a timeline of these experiences so that they have a fuller picture of how God was present to the disciples in the days before the Ascension. Use a phrase or symbol to represent each time Jesus was sighted, and notice the different ways and times he appeared to people. Ask family members to add a few examples of times in their lives that they have noticed Christ present.

June 9, 2019

Pentecost Sunday

Hearing the Word
John 14:15–16, 23b–26

In the name of the Father, and of the Son, and of the Holy Spirit.

Jesus said to his disciples: "If you love me, you will keep my commandments. And I will ask the Father, and he will give you another Advocate to be with you always.

"Whoever loves me will keep my word, and my Father will love him, and we will come to him and make our dwelling with him. Those who do not love me do not keep my words; yet the word you hear is not mine but that of the Father who sent me.

"I have told you this while I am with you. The Advocate, the Holy Spirit whom the Father will send in my name will teach you everything and remind you of all that I told you."

Reflecting on the Word

Come Spirit, come! The Church focuses on our love for God as we celebrate the fiery descent of the Spirit. The Gospel shows that our love for God is revealed in our keeping the Commandments and Jesus' Word. If we are unable to do those, our love for God is lacking. The Spirit is always with us to show us the way. It is good to reflect on how often we rely on the Holy Spirit to guide us.

······ ON THE WAY TO MASS

How does the fire of the Spirit live in you?

ON THE WAY HOME FROM MASS ······

What kind of fuel do you need to keep the fire of the Holy Spirit alive in your life?

Living the Word

If it is possible, build a fire in a fireplace, a barbecue grill, or if your city or town allows, in your backyard. An alternative is to light a number of candles. Around the flames of the fire or candles, name gifts that God has given you and say how you are going to feed that spark. The seven gifts of the Spirit are wisdom, understanding, counsel or right judgment, fortitude, knowledge, piety, and fear of the Lord.

June 16, 2019

Solemnity of the Most Holy Trinity

Hearing the Word

John 16:12–15

In the name of the Father, and of the Son, and of the Holy Spirit.

Jesus said to his disciples: "I have much more to tell you, but you cannot bear it now. But when he comes, the Spirit of truth, he will guide you to all truth. He will not speak on his own, but he will speak what he hears, and will declare to you the things that are coming. He will glorify me, because he will take from what is mine and declare it to you. Everything that the Father has is mine; for this reason I told you that he will take from what is mine and declare it to you."

Reflecting on the Word

Truth is a powerful thing that only exists in community. To be able to grasp the truth, you must hold the truth in relationship. God exists solely in relationship. The Father, the Son, and the Holy Spirit are always in relationship with one another. Being created in God's image, we are also called to constantly exist in relationship and seek the truth together.

······ ON THE WAY TO MASS

What is something you strongly believe to be true? How do you know it is true?

ON THE WAY HOME FROM MASS ······

Who are you in relationship with on a daily basis? How does that affect your decisions?

Living the Word

To help family members see how we are dependent upon one another, ask them each to draw a large outline of themselves and to divide the outline into different parts. Write the names of people who have influenced how you see things (eyes), have influenced your voice and what you say, or helped your ability to move (such as a coach or dance instructor). We are many parts but all one body. Notice if family members have any similarities or differences in who they feel connected to and how.

June 23, 2019

Solemnity of the Most Holy Body and Blood of Christ

Hearing the Word

Luke 9:11b–17

In the name of the Father, and of the Son, and of the Holy Spirit.

Jesus spoke to the crowds about the kingdom of God, and he healed those who needed to be cured. As the day was drawing to a close, the Twelve approached him and said, "Dismiss the crowd so that they can go to the surrounding villages and farms and find lodging and provisions; for we are in a deserted place here." He said to them, "Give them some food yourselves." They replied, "Five loaves and two fish are all we have, unless we ourselves go and buy food for all these people." Now the men there numbered about five thousand. Then he said to his disciples, "Have them sit down in groups of about fifty." They did so and made them all sit down. Then taking the five loaves and the two fish, and looking up to heaven, he said the blessing over them, broke them, and gave them to the disciples to set before the crowd. They all ate and were satisfied. And when the leftover fragments were picked up, they filled twelve wicker baskets.

Reflecting on the Word

We hear today that all of the people ate and were satisfied. At all-you-can-eat restaurants, it sometimes seems that no amount of food is enough. However, as Jesus fed people with his words, as well as with bread and fish, the people soon had their fill. Just like in the multiplication of the loaves and fish, we see in the Body of Christ, that God satisfies. When we truly know and rest in God's love, we realize we will always thirst and hunger for that infinite grace. Nothing is enough but this: to reside in the Body and Blood of Christ.

•••••• ON THE WAY TO MASS

What is something you can never seem to get enough of?

ON THE WAY HOME FROM MASS ••••••

Where do you see the Body of Christ in the flesh today?

Living the Word

Ask each family member to bring a favorite food to share at a picnic. Encourage them to notice how much fuller they feel when food is shared in love. When food is shared, we are fed in joy as well as in substance. As a result of the sharing of love and food we enjoy, we may feel full sooner. Invite your family to consider how this understanding can be incorporated into your daily meals.

June 30, 2019

Thirteenth Sunday in Ordinary Time

Hearing the Word

Luke 9:51–62

In the name of the Father, and of the Son, and of the Holy Spirit.

When the days for Jesus' being taken up were fulfilled, he resolutely determined to journey to Jerusalem, and he sent messengers ahead of him. On the way they entered a Samaritan village to prepare for his reception there, but they would not welcome him because the destination of his journey was Jerusalem. When the disciples James and John saw this they asked, "Lord, do you want us to call down fire from heaven to consume them?" Jesus turned and rebuked them, and they journeyed to another village.

As they were proceeding on their journey someone said to him, "I will follow you wherever you go." Jesus answered him, "Foxes have dens and birds of the sky have nests, but the Son of Man has nowhere to rest his head."

And to another he said, "Follow me." But he replied, "Lord, let me go first and bury my father." But he answered him, "Let the dead bury their dead. But you, go and proclaim the kingdom of God." And another said, "I will follow you, Lord, but first let me say farewell to my family at home." To him Jesus said, "No one who sets a hand to the plow and looks to what was left behind is fit for the kingdom of God."

Reflecting on the Word

At first glance this reading seems harsh, but Jesus' words portray the reality of discipleship. Following Jesus is the Christian's first priority, no matter the importance or worthiness of other matters and relationships. When God is first in our lives, all else will fall in place. What do you let get in the way of your vocation to follow the Lord?

• • • • • • ON THE WAY TO MASS

In the past, what have you put before God? Did you forget to say your bedtime prayers because you watched TV until too late?

ON THE WAY HOME FROM MASS • • • • • •

When was a time you put God first and it helped you accomplish something more easily?

Living the Word

Choose an afternoon for the family to put God first in an obvious way. Encourage each family member to say a prayer before each activity or to dedicate the activity to God in some way. While washing dishes or brushing teeth, you may thank God for dishes to wash or teeth to brush. Little children may need to pair up with someone older to help that person out. Encourage participants to notice if expressing gratitude changes how these tasks are done.

July 7, 2019

Fourteenth Sunday in Ordinary Time

Hearing the Word

Luke 10:1–12

In the name of the Father, and of the Son, and of the Holy Spirit.

At that time the Lord appointed seventy-two others whom he sent ahead of him in pairs to every town and place he intended to visit. He said to them, "The harvest is abundant but the laborers are few; so ask the master of the harvest to send out laborers for his harvest. Go on your way; behold, I am sending you like lambs among wolves. Carry no money bag, no sack, no sandals; and greet no one along the way. Into whatever house you enter, first say, 'Peace to this household.' If a peaceful person lives there, your peace will rest on him; but if not, it will return to you. Stay in the same house and eat and drink what is offered to you, for the laborer deserves his payment. Do not move about from one house to another. Whatever town you enter and they welcome you, eat what is set before you, cure the sick in it and say to them, 'The kingdom of God is at hand for you.' Whatever town you enter and they do not receive you, go out into the streets and say, 'The dust of your town that clings to our feet, even that we shake off against you.' Yet know this: the kingdom of God is at hand. I tell you, it will be more tolerable for Sodom on that day than for that town."

Reflecting on the Word

When Jesus sends his disciples out to spread his message, he gives specific instructions. He tells them not to carry a money bag so that they will be dependent on the hospitality of strangers. They are to accept the hospitality that is offered and to keep going when welcome is not extended. When they encounter peaceful people, the peace the disciples carry will be extended. These disciples who are sent out with nothing will need to rely completely on the Lord. When have you completely relied on God?

• • • • • • ON THE WAY TO MASS

What does it look like to send out peace? Where would you like peace to grow?

ON THE WAY HOME FROM MASS • • • • • •

How does a thought or idea take hold and spread?

Living the Word

With the family, create a visual for today's reading. Needed for the activity are a paper towel, washable markers, and water. Ask the children to use the markers to draw a picture on napkins to represent their good works. Explain that the water represents God's peace, and then dip the napkins in the water. Watch how much further the color goes when wet. God's peace enables good works to have a much further reach. When we come in peace, our message spreads more quickly and easily and can adapt to each situation.

July 14, 2019

Fifteenth Sunday in Ordinary Time

Hearing the Word

Luke 10:30–35

In the name of the Father, and of the Son, and of the Holy Spirit.

[Jesus said,] "A man fell victim to robbers as he went down from Jerusalem to Jericho. They stripped and beat him and went off leaving him half-dead. A priest happened to be going down that road, but when he saw him, he passed by on the opposite side. Likewise a Levite came to the place, and when he saw him, he passed by on the opposite side. But a Samaritan traveler who came upon him was moved with compassion at the sight. He approached the victim, poured oil and wine over his wounds and bandaged them. Then he lifted him up on his own animal, took him to an inn, and cared for him. The next day he took out two silver coins and gave them to the innkeeper with the instruction, 'Take care of him. If you spend more than what I have given you, I shall repay you on my way back.'"

Reflecting on the Word

Three people come upon a suffering man, and only the Samaritan is moved with compassion. The priest and the Levite may have had good reason to cross to the other side of the road, for they needed to keep clean for worship. But for right worship, the Lord demands justice and mercy. The Samaritan, who is looked down upon for worshipping at a place other than the Temple, shows the face of God to this nearly dead man.

......ON THE WAY TO MASS

Where is an area that you could bring more love to in your life, neighborhood, or world?

ON THE WAY HOME FROM MASS ......

Where do you expect goodness to occur?

Living the Word

Life is full of surprises. As a family, make a list of people that have caused hurt or pain in your life. Then, next to the names write down a list of good things that they have done. Give thanks for those good things, then pray for healing and growth in you and them to rectify the pain they have caused in your life. Help often comes from those that we least expect to provide it.

July 21, 2019

Sixteenth Sunday in Ordinary Time

Hearing the Word

Luke 10:38–42

In the name of the Father, and of the Son, and of the Holy Spirit.

Jesus entered a village where a woman whose name was Martha welcomed him. She had a sister named Mary who sat beside the Lord at his feet listening to him speak. Martha, burdened with much serving, came to him and said, "Lord, do you not care that my sister has left me by myself to do the serving? Tell her to help me." The Lord said to her in reply, "Martha, Martha, you are anxious and worried about many things. There is need of only one thing. Mary has chosen the better part and it will not be taken from her."

Reflecting on the Word

Where do worry and anxiety ever get us but away from the present? Jesus does not chastise Martha's hospitality or attention to detail but her inability to be present with him in the moment. In our lives, too, there are times to put aside our work to participate in graced moments. Consider whether you have passed by important moments because you were too busy.

······ ON THE WAY TO MASS

In what way was I too busy for God last week?

ON THE WAY HOME FROM MASS ······

What is one worry I could let go of, even if it is just for a day?

Living the Word

Gather the family and ask each member to pick a worry or concern and talk about how they feel when they think about it. Family members can describe the feeling with words or by how their body reacts when they think about the concern. They could also use a metaphor or color to describe the feeling. Then, ask each person to think of what it would feel like if that worry were given over to God for one day.

July 28, 2019

Seventeenth Sunday in Ordinary Time

Hearing the Word

Luke 11:1–13

In the name of the Father, and of the Son, and of the Holy Spirit.

Jesus was praying in a certain place, and when he had finished, one of his disciples said to him, "Lord, teach us to pray just as John taught his disciples." He said to them, "When you pray, say: / Father, hallowed be your name, / your kingdom come. / Give us each day our daily bread / and forgive us our sins / for we ourselves forgive everyone in debt to us, / and do not subject us to the final test."

And he said to them, "Suppose one of you has a friend to whom he goes at midnight and says, 'Friend, lend me three loaves of bread, for a friend of mine has arrived at my house from a journey and I have nothing to offer him,' and he says in reply from within, 'Do not bother me; the door has already been locked and my children and I are already in bed. I cannot get up to give you anything.' I tell you, if he does not get up to give the visitor the loaves because of their friendship, he will get up to give him whatever he needs because of his persistence.

"And I tell you, ask and you will receive; seek and you will find; knock and the door will be opened to you. For everyone who asks, receives; and the one who seeks, finds; and to the one who knocks, the door will be opened.

What father among you would hand his son a snake when he asks for a fish? Or hand him a scorpion when he asks for an egg? If you then, who are wicked, know how to give good gifts to your children, how much more will the Father in heaven give the Holy Spirit to those who ask him?"

Reflecting on the Word

If a child would request a fish, he would trust that his father would provide it. This reading helps us to consider our trust in God. Do we trust God enough to hand over our anxieties? Do we trust God enough that we would request what we need? Or do we rely on ourselves for everything we need?

......ON THE WAY TO MASS

What door do you want to knock on this week? What will you do if it opens?

ON THE WAY HOME FROM MASS ......

What is your favorite part of the Lord's Prayer and why?

Living the Word

As a family, write your version of the Lord's Prayer. Tailor it to your specific situation, time, and place. Perhaps rice is a staple in your family. If so, you might want to replace the word "bread" with "rice." The family might want to use another image for God that is found in the Bible. The family could consider a tune for singing the prayer. Try praying your new prayer at mealtime this week.

August 4, 2019

Eighteenth Sunday in Ordinary Time

Hearing the Word

Luke 12:13–21

In the name of the Father, and of the Son, and of the Holy Spirit.

Someone in the crowd said to Jesus, "Teacher, tell my brother to share the inheritance with me." He replied to him, "Friend, who appointed me as your judge and arbitrator?" Then he said to the crowd, "Take care to guard against all greed, for though one may be rich, one's life does not consist of possessions."

Then he told them a parable. "There was a rich man whose land produced a bountiful harvest. He asked himself, 'What shall I do, for I do not have space to store my harvest?' And he said, 'This is what I shall do: I shall tear down my barns and build larger ones. There I shall store all my grain and other goods and I shall say to myself, "Now as for you, you have so many good things stored up for many years, rest, eat, drink, be merry!"' But God said to him, 'You fool, this night your life will be demanded of you; and the things you have prepared, to whom will they belong?' Thus will it be for all who store up treasure for themselves but are not rich in what matters to God."

Reflecting on the Word

This man's treasure benefited no one. It did not help him, for he was going to die before he could use what he had stored. The treasure did not aid those who were in need because he did not offer it to them. The man was rich, but his wealth did him no good. We can consider whether we are rich in what matters to God or we invest in things that will do us no good.

......ON THE WAY TO MASS

What is something you want but you know you don't actually need?

ON THE WAY HOME FROM MASS ......

Do you know anyone who missed a meal because it could not be afforded? What might that feel like?

Living the Word

Walk through the neighborhood as a family looking out for the abundance that nature offers during this time of year. Encourage everyone to notice the variety of flowers and plants. If you live an area with farms and gardens, discuss who will eat the foods that are grown and how they get to the table. If your family has a garden, discuss whether you can bring some of the produce to a food pantry.

August 11, 2019

Nineteenth Sunday in Ordinary Time

Hearing the Word

Luke 12:32–40

In the name of the Father, and of the Son, and of the Holy Spirit.

Jesus said to his disciples: "Do not be afraid any longer, little flock, for your Father is pleased to give you the kingdom. Sell your belongings and give alms. Provide money bags for yourself that do not wear out, an inexhaustible treasure in heaven that no thief can reach nor moth destroy. For where your treasure is, there also will your heart be.

"Gird your loins and light your lamps and be like servants who await their master's return from a wedding, ready to open immediately when he comes and knocks. Blessed are those servants whom the master finds vigilant on his arrival. Amen, I say to you, he will gird himself, have them recline at table, and proceed to wait on them. And should he come in the second or third watch and find them prepared in this way, blessed are those servants. Be sure of this: if the master of the house had known the hour when the thief was coming, he would not have let his house be broken into. You also must be prepared, for at an hour you do not expect, the Son of Man will come."

Reflecting on the Word

We are called to not just wait idly for God's coming but to be in an active state of readiness. The disciples believed that God could be coming at any moment for the final days of earth. There was an excitement and expectancy to everything they did. In this day and age, surrounded by so much technology, the immediacy of God's ever-present love among us can seem to be lost. It is worthy to reflect on whether we are alert to God's presence.

......ON THE WAY TO MASS

What are you waiting for currently?

ON THE WAY HOME FROM MASS ......

What is the value of being bored? When was the last time you let yourself experience boredom?

Living the Word

Encourage the family to spend one day free of any screens or media outside of what is needed for work or school. Ask the family what it is like to go without their devices for a day. Is the home quieter? the pace slower? Is there more waiting? Without a screen to look at, what do they do while they are waiting? Discuss with the family whether they want to begin to have one screen-free day or evening weekly.

Solemnity of the Assumption of the Blessed Virgin Mary

Hearing the Word

Luke 1:39–55

In the name of the Father, and of the Son, and of the Holy Spirit.

Mary set out and traveled to the hill country in haste to a town of Judah, where she entered the house of Zechariah and greeted Elizabeth. When Elizabeth heard Mary's greeting, the infant leapt in her womb, and Elizabeth, filled with the Holy Spirit, cried out in a loud voice and said, "Blessed are you among women, and blessed is the fruit of your womb. And how does this happen to me, that the mother of my Lord should come to me? For at the moment the sound of your greeting reached my ears, the infant in my womb leaped for joy. Blessed are you who believed that what was spoken to you by the Lord would be fulfilled."

And Mary said: / "My soul proclaims the greatness of the Lord; / my spirit rejoices in God my Savior / for he has looked upon his lowly servant. / From this day all generations will call me blessed: / the Almighty has done great things for me, / and holy is his Name. / He has mercy on those who fear him / in every generation. / He has shown the strength of his arm, / and has scattered the proud in their conceit. / He has cast down the mighty from their thrones, / and has lifted up the lowly. / He has filled the hungry with good things, / and the rich he has sent away empty. / He has come to the help of his servant Israel / for he has remembered his promise of mercy, / the promise he made to our fathers, / to Abraham and his children forever."

Reflecting on the Word

As Mary meets Elizabeth, she sings the praises of God in a prayer that we now call the Magnificat. In this prayer, she tells of the good that God has done for her and her ancestors. Mary stands between the Old and New Testaments, between the old and new covenants. Her words tell of the fidelity, mercy, and compassion that God showed to her people and that he will continue to show to his followers.

• • • • • • ON THE WAY TO MASS

How do you praise God?

ON THE WAY HOME FROM MASS • • • • • •

Why is Mary described as "lowly" and what does that mean to you?

Living the Word

Mary calls herself "lowly" and attributes her carrying Jesus in her womb to God's goodness. Ask the family to find examples in the news of people who have achieved greatness, even though they are from a lowly background. Do you have family members or friends who have remarkable accomplishments but humbly never discuss them? Discuss what it means to give praise to God for the good things that happen to you.

Twentieth Sunday in Ordinary Time

Hearing the Word

Luke 12:49–53

In the name of the Father, and of the Son, and of the Holy Spirit.

Jesus said to his disciples: "I have come to set the earth on fire, and how I wish it were already blazing! There is a baptism with which I must be baptized, and how great is my anguish until it is accomplished! Do you think that I have come to establish peace on the earth? No, I tell you, but rather division. From now on a household of five will be divided, three against two and two against three; a father will be divided against his son and a son against his father, a mother against her daughter and a daughter against her mother, a mother-in-law against her daughter-in-law and a daughter-in-law against her mother-in-law."

Reflecting on the Word

It might seem alarming to some that Jesus says that he came to bring division, not peace. In today's reading, the cost of discipleship is noted. When one family member is on fire with the love of God, it can cost them relationships with others who refuse to acknowledge God. Followers of the Lord who are on fire with his love cannot be complacent. They will work for justice, mercy, and compassion. They will also be rejected by those whose priorities differ. No matter what occurs with earthly relationships, God's love is steadfast.

•••••• ON THE WAY TO MASS

When has standing up for love caused division in your life? What happened?

ON THE WAY HOME FROM MASS ••••••

What has God given you to burn in your heart?

Living the Word

With your children, role-play age-appropriate situations in which a person needs to stand up for God's love. Give the children scenarios and take turns playing each side of the situation. Talk about how easy or hard it is to stand up for love and how it feels to give in to the other side sometimes. Come up with specific phrases they can use in each situation. If children are ready with prepared statements, it is easier for them to go against what is popular. Ask your children if they have any situations they would like to explore further.

August 25, 2019

Twenty-First Sunday in Ordinary Time

Hearing the Word

Luke 13:22–30

In the name of the Father, and of the Son, and of the Holy Spirit.

Jesus passed through towns and villages, teaching as he went and making his way to Jerusalem. Someone asked him, "Lord, will only a few people be saved?" He answered them, "Strive to enter through the narrow gate, for many, I tell you, will attempt to enter but will not be strong enough. After the master of the house has arisen and locked the door, then will you stand outside knocking and saying, 'Lord, open the door for us.' He will say to you in reply, 'I do not know where you are from.' And you will say, 'We ate and drank in your company and you taught in our streets.' Then he will say to you, 'I do not know where you are from. Depart from me, all you evildoers!' And there will be wailing and grinding of teeth when you see Abraham, Isaac and Jacob and all the prophets in the kingdom of God and you yourselves cast out. And people will come from the east and the west and from the north and the south and will recline at table in the kingdom of God. For behold, some are last who will be first, and some are first who will be last."

Reflecting on the Word

Nothing is a given. Jesus reminds us that while God's love and salvation are open to all, many find it hard to accept them. The Kingdom of God requires an active engagement on our part. We must choose. As soon as we become complacent, refusing to be on fire with his love, our path to be with him in eternity can slip away. Jesus is always calling us to vigilance. If we don't intend to keep the Lord's ways, we cannot expect to be part of the feast in the Kingdom of God.

······ ON THE WAY TO MASS

How can you be more intentional about your love for God?

ON THE WAY HOME FROM MASS ······

What did you almost miss during Mass because you weren't present in the moment?

Living the Word

Practice intentionality for an afternoon this weekend. Ask family members to pick a task they often do but to perform it more intentionally and deliberately. These tasks could be setting the table, making their bed, completing a homework assignment, or even reading aloud. Encourage them to notice how being intentional changes the task and enhances the experience.

September 1, 2019

Twenty-Second Sunday in Ordinary Time

Hearing the Word

Luke 14:1, 7–14

In the name of the Father, and of the Son, and of the Holy Spirit.

On a sabbath Jesus went to dine at the home of one of the leading Pharisees. . . .

He told a parable to those who had been invited, noticing how they were choosing the places of honor at the table. "When you are invited by someone to a wedding banquet, do not recline at table in the place of honor. A more distinguished guest than you may have been invited by him, and the host who invited both of you may approach you and say, 'Give your place to this man,' and then you would proceed with embarrassment to take the lowest place. Rather, when you are invited, go and take the lowest place so that when the host comes to you he may say, 'My friend, move up to a higher position.' Then you will enjoy the esteem of your companions at the table. For everyone who exalts himself will be humbled, but the one who humbles himself will be exalted." Then he said to the host who invited him, "When you hold a lunch or a dinner, do not invite your friends or your brothers or your relatives or your wealthy neighbors, in case they may invite you back and you have repayment. Rather, when you hold a banquet, invite the poor, the crippled, the lame, the blind; blessed indeed will you be because of their inability to repay you. For you will be repaid at the resurrection of the righteous."

Reflecting on the Word

It is common to expect reciprocity. We are likely to invite people to lunch or to our homes if they have extended an invitation to us. Jesus is asking for a different way of being when he says that those who cannot repay should be asked to the banquet. We can consider that God invites us to the heavenly banquet and we can never repay him.

•••••• ON THE WAY TO MASS

Can you think of a time when you were humbled? What happened then? Are you able to laugh about it now?

ON THE WAY HOME FROM MASS ••••••

What does it mean to be exalted in God's eyes?

Living the Word

The last shall be first. Talk with your family about how they have felt when they have allowed another to go first. Ask if it gave them a certain sense of contentment. Under what circumstances have they allowed others to go first? Could they do this more often? Encourage family members to seek to be last instead for a day. During this day, have fun play-fully reversing the order on everything and even eating dessert first.

EVERYDAY FAMILY PRAYERS

The Sign of the Cross

The Sign of the Cross is the first prayer and the last: of each day, and of each Christian life. It is a prayer of the body as well as a prayer of words. When we are presented for Baptism, the community traces this sign on our bodies for the first time. Parents may trace it daily on their children. We learn to trace it daily on ourselves and on those whom we love. When we die, our loved ones will trace this holy sign on us for the last time.

In the name of the Father,

and of the Son,

and of the Holy Spirit. Amen.

The Lord's Prayer

The Lord's Prayer, or the Our Father, is a very important prayer for Christians because Jesus himself taught it to his disciples, who taught it to his Church. Today, we say this prayer as part of Mass, in the Rosary, and in personal prayer. There are seven petitions in the Lord's Prayer. The first three ask for God to be glorified and praised, and the next four ask for God to help take care of our physical and spiritual needs.

Our Father, who art in heaven,

hallowed be thy name;

thy kingdom come,

thy will be done

on earth as it is in heaven.

Give us this day our daily bread,

and forgive us our trespasses,

as we forgive those who trespass against us;

and lead us not into temptation, but deliver us from evil.

The Apostles' Creed

The Apostles' Creed is one of the earliest creeds we have; scholars believe it was written within the second century. The Apostles' Creed is shorter than the Nicene Creed, but it states what we believe about the Father, Son, and Holy Spirit. This prayer is sometimes used at Mass, especially at Masses with children, and is part of the Rosary.

I believe in God,

the Father almighty,

Creator of heaven and earth,

and in Jesus Christ, his only Son, our Lord,

who was conceived by the Holy Spirit,

born of the Virgin Mary,

suffered under Pontius Pilate,

was crucified, died and was buried;

he descended into hell;

and on the third day he rose again from the dead;

he ascended into heaven,

and is seated at the right hand of God the Father almighty;

from there he will come to judge the living and the dead.

I believe in the Holy Spirit,

the holy catholic Church,

the communion of saints,

the forgiveness of sins,

the resurrection of the body,

and life everlasting. Amen.

The Nicene Creed

The Nicene Creed was written at the Council of Nicaea in AD 325, when bishops of the Church gathered together in order to articulate true belief in who Christ is and in his relationship to God the Father. The Nicene Creed was the final document of that Council, written so that all the faithful may know the central teachings of Christianity. We say this prayer at Mass.

I believe in one God,

the Father almighty,

maker of heaven and earth,

of all things visible and invisible.

I believe in one Lord Jesus Christ,

the Only Begotten Son of God,

born of the Father before all ages.

God from God, Light from Light,

true God from true God,

begotten, not made, consubstantial with the Father;

through him all things were made.

For us men and for our salvation

he came down from heaven,

and by the Holy Spirit was incarnate of the Virgin Mary,

and became man.

For our sake he was crucified under Pontius Pilate,

he suffered death and was buried,

and rose again on the third day

in accordance with the Scriptures.
He ascended into heaven
and is seated at the right hand of the Father.
He will come again in glory
to judge the living and the dead
and his kingdom will have no end.

I believe in the Holy Spirit, the Lord, the giver of life,
who proceeds from the Father and the Son,
who with the Father and Son is adored and glorified,
who has spoken through the prophets.

I believe in one holy, catholic, and apostolic Church.
I confess one Baptism for the forgiveness of sins
and I look forward to the resurrection of the dead
and the life of the world to come. Amen.

Glory Be (Doxology)

This is a short prayer that Christians sometimes add to the end of psalms. It is prayed during the Rosary and usually follows the opening verse during the Liturgy of the Hours. It can be prayed at any time during the day.

Glory be to the Father

and to the Son

and to the Holy Spirit,

as it was in the beginning

is now, and ever shall be

world without end. Amen.

Hail Mary

The first two lines of this prayer are the words of the angel Gabriel to Mary, when he announces that she is with child (Luke 1:28). The second two lines are Elizabeth's greeting to Mary (Luke 1:42). The last four lines come to us from deep in history, from where and from whom we do not know. This prayer is part of the Rosary and is often used by Christians for personal prayer.

Hail, Mary, full of grace,

the Lord is with thee.

Blessed art thou among women

and blessed is the fruit of thy womb, Jesus.

Holy Mary, Mother of God,

pray for us sinners,

now and at the hour of our death.

Amen.

Reflecting on the Word

With the many details of our daily routines, it is easy for the heart to seem asleep to the signs of God in our lives. This first Gospel of the Advent season calls us to be alert to how God calls us. Christmas preparations should include taking time to examine what is most important in our lives. It is valuable to reflect on whether God is at the center of our family's life. We cannot let the anxieties of daily life take our eyes off our Lord.

......ON THE WAY TO MASS

When does your heart feel the most awake?

ON THE WAY HOME FROM MASS ......

What is your favorite part of the Advent season? What do you like most about it?

Living the Word

The First Sunday of Advent is a good time to establish your family's routine for the season. If you do not have an Advent wreath, you might want to set a candle on the table and say a simple prayer with your family asking for God's help so that each of you prepare your hearts for him. Invite family members to make petitions for people who need their prayers.

SOLEMNITY OF THE IMMACULATE CONCEPTION OF THE BLESSED VIRGIN MARY

Hearing the Word

Luke 1:26–38

In the name of the Father, and of the Son, and of the Holy Spirit.

The angel Gabriel was sent from God to a town of Galilee called Nazareth, to a virgin betrothed to a man named Joseph, of the house of David, and the virgin's name was Mary. And coming to her, he said, "Hail, full of grace! The Lord is with you." But she was greatly troubled at what was said and pondered what sort of greeting this might be. Then the angel said to her, "Do not be afraid, Mary, for you have found favor with God. Behold you will conceive in your womb and bear a son, and you shall name him Jesus. He will be great and will be called Son of the Most High, and the Lord God will give him the throne of David his father, and he will rule over the house of Jacob forever, and of his Kingdom there will be no end." But Mary said to the angel, "How can this be, since I have no relations with a man?" And the angel said to her in reply, "The Holy Spirit will come upon you, and the power of the Most High will overshadow you. Therefore the child to be born will be called holy, the Son of God. And behold, Elizabeth, your relative, has also conceived a son in her old age, and this is the sixth month for her who was called barren; for nothing will be impossible for God." Mary said, "Behold, I am the handmaid of the Lord. May it be done to me according to your word." Then the angel departed from her.

Reflecting on the Word

Mary's fiat, or total giving of self to the will of God, was a courageous act that showed her trust in God. As we look at others' lives, we may see that their yes to God may have come with a social or professional cost.

• • • • • • ON THE WAY TO MASS

What is something that would be hard for you to say yes to? What would people think if you did?

ON THE WAY HOME FROM MASS • • • • • •

The angel Gabriel is known as God's messenger. What message do you think the angel would have for you?

Living the Word

Talk with your children about how guardian angels can be called on during times of need. Ask the children to describe or draw what they imagine their angel looks like and what colors they wear. Explain that angels are special helpers for God. Tell them that angels watch over us now and will guide us when we return to heaven. Encourage them to add their guardian angel to daily prayers.

December 9, 2018

Second Sunday of Advent

Hearing the Word
Luke 3:1–6

In the name of the Father, and of the Son, and of the Holy Spirit.

In the fifteenth year of the reign of Tiberius Caesar, when Pontius Pilate was governor of Judea, and Herod was tetrarch of Galilee, and his brother Philip tetrarch of the region of Ituraea and Trachonitis, and Lysanias was tetrarch of Abilene, during the high priesthood of Annas and Caiaphas, the word of God came to John the son of Zechariah in the desert. John went throughout the whole region of the Jordan, proclaiming a baptism of repentance for the forgiveness of sins, as it is written in the book of the words of the prophet Isaiah: / *A voice of one crying out in the desert: / "Prepare the way of the Lord, / make straight his paths. / Every valley shall be filled / and every mountain and hill shall be made low. / The winding roads shall be made straight, / and the rough ways made smooth, / and all flesh shall see the salvation of God."*

Grace before Meals

Families pray before meals in different ways. Some families make up a prayer in their own words, other families sing a prayer, and many families use this traditional formula. Teach your children to say this prayer while signing themselves with the cross.

Bless us, O Lord, and these thy gifts,

which we are about to receive from thy bounty,

through Christ our Lord.

Amen.

Grace after Meals

Teach your children to say this prayer after meals, while signing themselves with the cross. The part in brackets is optional.

We give thee thanks, for all thy benefits,

almighty God, who lives and reigns forever.

[And may the souls of the faithful departed,

through the mercy of God, rest in peace.]

Amen.